-2

#WHATIS

#WHATIS
HYPNOSIS?

TOM FORTES MAYER

This edition first published in the UK and USA 2016 by
Watkins, an imprint of Watkins Media Limited
19 Cecil Court
London WC2N 4EZ

enquiries@watkinspublishing.com

Design and typography copyright © Watkins Media Limited 2016

Text copyright © Tom Fortes Mayer 2016

Tom Fortes Mayer has asserted his right under the Copyright, Designs
and Patents Act 1988 to be identified as the author of this work.

1 3 5 7 9 10 8 6 4 2

Typeset by Manisha Patel

Printed and bound in Germany

A CIP record for this book is available from the British Library

ISBN: 978-178028-930-4

www.watkinspublishing.com

CONTENTS

Why read this book?

This book is designed to give you a clear understanding of – and debunk many myths about – the fascinating world of hypnosis. When hypnosis is used in the best way it really is a beautiful tool for creating wonderful changes in your life.

When you are under hypnosis, you normally feel calm, relaxed and more open to suggestion. It is a trance-like state in which your focus and concentration are both heightened. It is not a complicated procedure. Nor does it require any special preparation, though you should be well-rested and wearing comfortable clothing to help you to relax fully. It is something you can do for yourself as well as through working with a hypnotherapist.

20 reasons to start reading!

Here are just some of the benefits you can gain from using hypnosis techniques.

1 Learn how to relax and unwind fully
2 Feel more confident, positive and enthusiastic about life
3 Increase health, vitality and energy
4 Enjoy sleeping more easily and fully
5 Enhance your creativity, increasing innovation and output
6 Be your best by increasing efficiency and excellence
7 Understand yourself and others more easily
8 Communicate more powerfully with yourself and others

9   Be a more powerful and effective leader

10 Be healthier and enjoy exercising more

11 Be more playful and spontaneous

12 Be more resilient in the face of difficulty

13 Be more emotionally stable

14 Reduce fears, anxieties and self-doubt

15 Reduce risks of mental health issues

16 Increase self-awareness and self- acceptance

17 Connect more to your purpose and enjoy a greater
    sense of meaning

18 Increase feelings of self-worth and fulfilment

19 Enjoy more connection with your loved ones

20 Enjoy more overall success and happiness in your life

As you can see from this list, hypnosis can really help you to
get the most out of your life and so enjoy it all the more. This
book will give you everything you need to understand the
principles and practices of hypnosis so that you can begin
using them to good effect on yourself – and maybe even on
some close friends and family. It will also make clear what to
expect if you choose to work with a qualified hypnotherapist,
including the many benefits this could bring into your life.

Key features of this book

In the introduction I explain why I am passionate about
hypnosis and why it is such a valuable subject to learn more

about. In Chapter 1, I give an overview of the history and development of hypnosis while debunking some myths along the way. In Chapter 2 I explain how hypnosis actually works and show you how to put its principles into practice. Chapter 3 details the purposes of hypnosis and highlights its wide variety of applications. Chapter 4 delves more deeply into how hypnosis can change your life and looks at the most powerful hypnotic techniques. Chapter 5 gives you a set of tools to enable you to use self-hypnosis to improve your everyday life. Chapter 6 looks at the wider social benefits of more people learning about the far-reaching power of hypnosis and putting its principles into practice.

The book is designed to make hypnosis as accessible as possible with the help of the following features:

- A Q & A approach that chapter by chapter answers the questions that are often asked about hypnosis
- 'Try it' exercises that give you a chance to experiment with hypnosis while you read
- 'Focus On' boxes that give additional information about the mind and how it works
- At the end of the book, a 'What Next?' section, including a further reading list, suggests how to continue your investigations into this fascinating subject and become more proficient in your practice.

SOME KEY TERMS

Affirmations Positive suggestions given through hypnosis

Conscious The logical, reasoning, decision-making part of the mind

Hypnotherapy Hypnosis used by a therapist as a primary tool for helping subjects to achieve their goals

Induction The technique of hypnotizing a person

Pacing Mimicking someone's posture, behaviour or language in order to help build rapport (see below)

Post-hypnotic suggestion A suggestion made while a person is in hypnosis to be acted on later

Progressive relaxation A technique used to progressively relax the entire body by focusing on individual areas in turn

Rapport The relationship between therapist and client in which the client has trust and confidence in the therapist and the therapist has concern for the client

Script A prewritten script that a therapist will use during trance work

Subconscious The part of the mind that is mostly below the level of our awareness

Trance state A state of consciousness when a person's attention is focused and they tend not to be so aware of external stimuli as a result

INTRODUCTION

Why this subject?

Hypnosis is a hugely misunderstood subject. In the simplest terms I like to think of it as the art and science of having an amazing day. Sometimes you wake up feeling happy, confident and on top of the world. People respond well to you, you enjoy what you are doing and everything seems to flow seamlessly. In contrast, there are those awful days that start badly and then continue to deteriorate. Everything is a struggle, you experience frustration, resentment and annoyance, and nothing seems to work for you.

This is where hypnosis can help you. Your state of mind affects everything you do, but you are most likely not aware of the extraordinary things that can be done to alter it, to enable you to make the most of every single day. This is what hypnosis is all about. More than that, it is about connecting you to your inner potential.

There are countless stories of human beings doing amazing things in emergencies. Tales of mothers lifting cars off their children, people jumping out of windows during fires and surviving incredible falls are just a few examples. There are also stories of extraordinary bravery and courage where people put themselves at considerable risk to save the lives of others. Deep down, you know that, if you had to, there is great potential waiting deep inside you.

You, like all of us, possess a fierce capacity to protect those that you love and a likely willingness to run terrifying risks if you are faced with a life-and-death situation. In such a moment, you can feel those reserves of capability waiting to be released. But why do you have to wait for an emergency to be your most amazing and inspiring self?

So many people coast along knowing that at best they are putting in maybe 60 per cent effort. If you have half a brain and you put in this amount of effort, you will most likely be performing well enough to be considered a valuable employee, a good family member and a lovable partner. And yet, you only get one chance at life.

Surely it would be worthwhile exploring the tools and techniques that will enable you to connect to your greatest potential? Think how it would help you to bring out your very best, so that you can make the most of every single moment of life? How would it feel access the kind of power that otherwise you would connect with only in an emergency? How might your life be different if you were 30 per cent more effective at work, at home, in love and in general life? What if there was a source of intelligence, efficiency and excellence within you that could enable you to perform way better than you could have previously imagined without having to put in more effort? Wouldn't that be worth exploring?

This is what hypnosis offers. Through it, you will be able to access the vast storehouse of brilliance and intelligence that lies within you. It is a natural, easy process that can help to alter how you think and feel, change what you believe and, ultimately, ensure that you are happier and more successful.

People try hard to improve their lives, but most of this effort is usually focussed on externals. People buy more gadgets and toys, they move home, or they constantly decorate or renovate. They take up more hobbies or go to see more shows. And they invest thousands in learning business strategies or practical things to do differently. Yet all the while they don't take the time to look at how they are using their minds. The thoughts, feelings, beliefs and behaviours we are all operating with affect everything that we do. So many people have achieved incredible things and have seen and experienced everything the world has to offer and yet they still feel hollow on the inside. Happiness and success are totally determined by our inner, not our outer, world.

Hypnosis is an incredible tool that you can start using yourself today to help you understand how you are thinking and feeling, what you are believing and why you are behaving the way you are. Hypnosis also enables you to make the vital changes to your thoughts, feelings, beliefs and behaviours so that you can transform your life from the inside out.

Why me?

A Harley Street hypnotherapist, I have been in private practice since 2000. I am endlessly fascinated by the power of the mind, the ways in which you can change how you think, feel and behave and the wonderful variety of tools and techniques that can help you decide to change your life for the better.

A huge epiphany changed my life in an instant, and it was that experience that led me to dedicate my life to understanding more deeply the mechanics of beliefs and what can be done to change them. Over the years, I have been able to refine my understanding of what hypnosis really is and how it actually works. More than that, I have seen time and time again the immense power it has for unlocking people's potential and putting them in touch with their natural desire to create more meaningful, purposeful lives.

I have treated a huge spectrum of people from across society: people who are really struggling with life, stuck in negative thought patterns and trapped by overwhelming emotions and crippling fears; celebrities, business leaders and world-class sportspeople who want to keep excelling at what they do. I have taught self-hypnosis to people all over the world and in a variety of settings. This work has taken me to Nigeria to reduce corruption, into prisons to reduce re-offending and into schools to increase engagement. Time and time again I have seen that hypnosis is an invaluable tool that can help people deeply transform their lives.

In my experience when people start connecting more with their inner mind using hypnosis, they become more beautiful people, and I have mapped that journey so many times that I feel I am a uniquely informed and incredibly enthusiastic guide. I hope that through this book I can share my passion for hypnosis with you so that you, too, can start to enjoy its broad range of benefits in your life.

Why now?

Primarily thanks to stage shows, hypnosis is often widely misunderstood by the general public. It is time to set the record straight and protect and preserve the integrity of this beautiful art form. Plus, due to the availability of downloadable hypnosis recordings and a whole range of online support tools, I can now provide you with everything you need to actively explore this wonderful world.

This book and its associated website www.freemind.org give you the tools to:

- Experience being hypnotized
- Learn how to hypnotize yourself

- Practise and use scripts to hypnotize others
- Combine self-hypnosis with music to be more effective
- Use hypnosis to enjoy more happiness and success

More than ever in today's world, there is the need for you to take control of your own psychology. To become very aware of the overt and covert messages that you are being bombarded with on a daily basis so that you can choose how you are being influenced. By doing this, you can start to have much greater control over how you live and how you feel. All true happiness comes from understanding who you are and why you make the choices that you do. Hypnosis can help you become much more objective about what you actually want and what will really make you truly happy, so I hope you enjoy the journey of exploration that the following pages will take you on.

What you should always bear in mind is that, whatever it is used for, hypnosis is a safe and effective process. It enables you to deal with your own mental challenges and blocks, so you can build on your strengths and take control of your destiny. It can be particularly helpful in resolving problems that you are finding hard to tackle. As you progress, I'm confident you will come to appreciate just what hypnosis has to offer and how it can help you to unleash your full potential in making the most of your life.

CHAPTER 1
What lies at the core of hypnosis?

Hypnosis revolves around changing beliefs, feelings, thoughts and behaviours. As you are reading this book, you are doing so with a number of beliefs embedded in your psychology. These might be beliefs about how good you are at maths, how easy you find getting up in the morning, beliefs about money and people that have lots of it, beliefs about relationships and the opposite sex and so on.

You may feel generally positive about most parts of your life, yet you may still be holding onto negative feelings about other aspects of it. You will have varying feelings about the different people in your life, too. While much of that may be very positive, you may still be holding onto frustrations or resentments about people you will never see again. While all of this is going on, it is most likely that you also have a set of behaviours and habits that you have mixed feelings about. You may be very proud of how dedicated you are at work or how you relate to some of your family members, but there will be some habits or ways of being that frustrate you about yourself.

Hypnosis helps you to look at this and the identity you are operating with, and gives you the tools to change it. However, this is not about becoming someone different or new. It is simply about reclaiming who you really are. So much of who we are and how we do things comes from the conditioning we have received from our parents, family, schools and culture, plus the ideas and beliefs of friends and colleagues. All of this has a huge impact on what we believe and what we expect. It is also very important to consider the huge impact that the world of advertising has on us, which can have a very detrimental effect on what we think and how we feel about ourselves. All of these elements are powerful conditioning forces that will make us think, feel, believe and behave in a certain way.

Hypnosis is the mechanism by which you can stop for a moment and truly feel into how all of that is working for you. It enables you to let go of ideas and identities that no longer serve you and instead helps you to start to rebuild thoughts and feelings about yourself that will enable you to enjoy lots of positive changes in your life.

How is hypnosis defined and what is its main aim?

Hypnosis is any process by which you access and influence your unconscious mind. Most commonly, it is used to deepen understanding, enhance emotional stability and unleash potential, thereby increasing the ability to enjoy life by operating more effectively and harmoniously. Technically, it is thought to work by turning off the analytical left-hand side of the brain while the unconscious right-hand side becomes more alert and aware of what is going on around it.

Commonly, hypnosis is used in the following circumstances:

- To help improve eating patterns and assist in weight management.
- To break the cycle of addictions, such as alcohol, drugs, sugar and what therapists term 'busy-ness'.
- To help with physical disorders, such as eczema, migraines and irritable bowel syndrome.
- To help with emotional problems, such as uncontrollable anger, anxiety and depression.
- To aid in the reduction or elimination of phobias.
- To help reduce stress and enhance relaxation.
- To help enhance life in general.

Is hypnosis safe and natural?

Contrary to what some people think, hypnosis is actually a simple and natural trance state that we all go in and out of every day. Examples include when we first wake up in the morning and are naturally groggy, or those times we are doing a menial task and start daydreaming or enter a state of reverie. On such occasions, we feel as if we are a million miles away. Some people, most notably athletes, refer to this as 'zoning out'. Likewise, drivers making a routine journey often cannot really remember making any conscious decisions about their driving during it. They have been driving more or less on autopilot.

Most people are unaware of what a powerful opportunity we have to induce and harness such trance states to help us think, feel, believe and behave differently. In moments of entrancement like this, it is possible to direct our thinking in much more positive ways. We can introduce new beliefs, dissolve limiting thinking and encourage new behaviours. We can become much more objective about our emotions, access new levels of insight and unleash new levels of personal and professional excellence.

Does hypnosis involve giving over control to someone else?

I truly believe that hypnosis is one of the greatest tools available to help you love your life even more. Yet many people are afraid of it. Primarily, they hate the notion that being hypnotized might mean giving over control to the person doing the hypnosis.

This is a popular misconception. Hypnosis is in no way about forcing people to do anything against their will. Neither is it about exerting control over people or turning them into something they do not want to be. In fact, it is quite the opposite. You remain in control throughout.

Let's assume you are working with a hypnotherapist to make this happen. In such a case, the therapist will be trying anything and everything he or she can to influence you as part of helping you find your own way to recognize, and release, your greatest potential.

What actually goes on in the mind?

When we think, the mind turns over thoughts at a certain rate. This is measured in Hertz, commonly shortened to Hz. When you are extremely excited, in a state of panic, or simply concentrating deeply, your thought frequency is between 40 Hz and 100 Hz. This produces what are termed Gamma waves. The normal thought frequency is between 12 Hz and 40 Hz. This produces Beta waves. As we drift into relaxation or the beginning of sleep, the mind slows further. The thought frequency drops to between 8 Hz to 12 Hz with Alpha waves being produced as a result.

Differing brainwaves

Alpha waves open up the bridge between conscious and unconscious thought. It is these brainwaves we are experiencing when we move in and out of simple hypnotic trance states during the day. I call this relaxed entrancement, which can be very useful when we want to change how we think, feel, believe and behave.

When hypnosis becomes even more powerful, however, it induces an even slower frequency. The mind slows to between 4 and 8 Hz and starts to produce so-called Theta waves. These are connected with deep daydreaming and experiencing and feeling raw emotions. They also stimulate intuition and creativity as well as increasing natural feelings of harmony and health. Using deep hypnosis, it is possible to access this way of thinking while remaining completely conscious. Below 4 Hz is the realm of Delta brainwaves and this is the frequency of deep restorative sleep.

By simply slowing down your mind, you are able to access deeper levels of relaxation, creativity and insight. You will find that you are able to release repressed emotions, increase personal awareness and unleash your potential. In later chapters, I will discuss how this is done in more detail. At this stage it is simply important to be very clear that hypnosis is a natural mental state and that for thousands of years people have been utilizing a variety of hypnotic techniques (although they weren't called that) to access the power of the unconscious mind.

From these examples, we can see that at least some of the most ancient roots of the healing professions were grounded in practices that explored the hinterland of consciousness that exists around the edge of sleep. It is there that we can finally become conscious of that which was previously unconscious and resolve our challenges.

How did hypnosis develop?

The origins of hypnosis stretch far back into history. It is referred to obliquely in the Bible and the ancient Hindus, Chinese, Egyptians and Greeks all seem to have known of it. In the late 1700s, Franz Anton Mesmer popularized what became known as mesmerism; the following century, James Braid, a Scottish doctor, coined the word hypnosis, taken from the Greek god of sleep Hypnos, to describe the process. Other notable pioneers include the French neurologist Jean-Martin Charcot, his pupil Pierre Janet and Émil Coué, a brilliant French psychologist.

In modern times, the world's greatest hypnotist was undoubtedly an American psychiatrist called Milton Erickson, who lived from 1901 to 1980. Before his time, hypnosis was dictatorial and directive. Earlier hypnotherapists were more like sergeant-majors, giving orders. This approach is called 'authoritarian' and 'direct'.

It worked like this. Once the subject was in a hypnotic trance, a hypnotherapist would repeat suggestions over and over in very forceful tones. He or she would give 'direct' suggestions such as 'You have no desire to smoke', or 'You will wake up tomorrow feeling good and always eat the right amount of the right kind of foods'. Still to this day, many hypnotists use these authoritarian and direct approaches. At certain stages of the hypnotic process, these are very effective, but at others they can provoke rebellion and resistance. Many people do not respond well to being told what to do and you cannot always deal directly with the 'problem'. Nor will a 'problem' commonly co-operate with its own dissolution.

Erickson therefore decided to develop different ways of encouraging people to change their beliefs. He developed a style that is now called 'permissive' and 'indirect'. Instead of telling people they were going into hypnosis and directing them to feel relaxed, Erickson would invite people simply to notice that they were becoming relaxed. He would invite and encourage people to become more aware of relaxation moving through their body. This permissive style is collaborative and leading as opposed to dictatorial and controlling, which means subjects are far less likely to resist and rebel when the technique is skilfully employed.

Erickson then took this much further. He developed an extraordinary power to help people by mastering the art of metaphor. He knew that metaphor could bypass the conscious mind completely. If, for example, someone was coming to him complaining about lack of confidence, he wouldn't mention confidence at all. He would instead talk about growing tomatoes and about them needing the right amount of sun and soil, and the correct kind of nutritious and

TRYIT SIMPLE RELAXATION

This exercise introduces you to one of the most basic principles on which hypnosis relies. Learning how to relax is a fundamental part of the process. With practice, it is a relatively easy state to achieve.

1 Sit in a comfortable position and find something to stare at. Take a moment to become completely still.

2 Soften and relax the stare. Then start to stare into the distance as though you were looking out to sea, while at the same time maintaining awareness of the space before the point on which you are focusing. Also try to be aware of everything else your eyes can see, even though you are not actually looking at it.

3 Choose your moment to become totally transfixed. Then slow down your breathing, making each breath last for as long as possible. Allow your eyelids to feel tired and try to induce your vision to blur slightly.

4 Gently close your eyes and rest in total stillness, simply noticing relaxation flowing through your body. Do this for as long as it feels good.

fertile elements. He would talk about the person caring for the tomatoes, ensuring that they got the right amount of water and sunlight. This metaphorical approach can be far more effective than directing people to change – it empowers subjects more strongly in the long run as they are much more likely to feel they have created the changes for themselves.

Crafting an effective metaphor or visualization for a subject can be incredibly complicated, but is useful because so much therapeutic ground can be covered in an incredibly short amount of time. When it is done skilfully the impact can be so strong that it leaves you in awe-filled amazement.

These metaphorical styles of hypnosis work best when combined with a very deep level of relaxation, but they can be employed in any conversation to help paint a picture or convey more meaning in a shorter period of time. If a picture is better than a thousand words, then a good metaphor is more powerful than ten thousand words.

Will you remain conscious when you are hypnotized?

Given that people have seen stage hypnotists tap a volunteer on the shoulder, and seemingly put them to sleep by theatrically giving them a command, it is understandable that there is substantial confusion about hypnosis. While it is common to enter into a light hypnotic trance state before falling asleep and again when first waking up, hypnosis is absolutely not about sleeping.

When we are hypnotized, we have not gone to sleep, we are not in some faraway kingdom and we have not fallen under the power of the hypnotist. We remain fully conscious, in control and can snap out of the trance at any time.

In 1991, Dr Stephen H Wolinsky, a celebrated American hypnotist and meditation teacher, wrote a remarkable book called *Trances People Live*. In it, he suggested that actually we are all walking around in a trance. We are stuck on automatic pilot in our various personal, professional and social roles. We think of ourselves as a certain kind of person, a son, a daughter, a mother or father, we think of ourselves as successful or not, as attractive or not, we relate to life as though it is easy or hard, enjoyable or depressing. Wolinsky suggests that all of these ideas and identities keep us locked in a trance. He says, and I agree, that hypnosis is a way of coming out of a trance. It is a way of dissolving the conditioning and truly becoming who we really are. Hypnosis at its best is not about going to sleep – it is about waking up.

How important is relaxation in hypnosis?

The human body cannot be relaxed and afraid at the same time. If you think about something you are afraid of, you will start to tense your body. One of the main ways in which hypnosis can change your life is to use it to enter into a very deeply relaxed state. Once you are in that peaceful and calm state, you are able to think about things that previously would have scared you without becoming tense. You can also utilize the relaxation hypnosis brings and direct it toward any areas of tension or disease in your body. This has been proven to aid in pain management and with the healing process. It can also be used to help you feel relaxed enough to be willing to explore old thoughts and feelings that may once have been very painful or scary. Relaxation, in short, gives you the confidence to deal with difficult feelings and put them behind you once and for all.

This level of hypnotic relaxation can be used to heal the full gamut of fear-based conditions. Whether that is helping you dissolve phobias, overcome shyness, beat full-on anxiety attacks or simply enabling you to deliver a presentation or speech with much more confidence, hypnosis can bring a level of peace to every level of your being.

How does hypnosis differ from hypnotherapy?

Hypnosis is an umbrella term for any practice involving connecting with a person's unconscious mind to exert an ideally positive influence. Hypnotherapy is somewhat different. Specifically, it is about using hypnosis to help people overcome difficulties, achieve goals and enjoy greater levels of health, happiness and harmony.

Because the state of hypnosis allows a person to access the power of the unconscious it is possible to employ it to accelerate many forms of therapeutic practices. Through gaining direct access to the unconscious mind, things can be understood more rapidly, unconscious motivations that may be driving negative behaviour can be accessed more easily, and new suggestions for more harmonious behaviours can be absorbed and adopted more effectively.

Anxiety, depression, phobias, addictions, self-esteem issues, confidence issues, weight loss, irritable bowel syndrome, tinnitus, sleep disorders, anger issues, skin conditions, negative thinking, stress management and many other conditions can all be treated successfully with hypnotherapy. It is also used extensively in the field of peak performance where top sportspeople, artists, sales people, presenters and entertainers use principles and techniques to bring out their best performance.

What happens in a hypnotherapy session?

Most hypnotherapists suggest an initial consultation, generally lasting around an hour. It usually involves the following areas of discussion:

- Your requirements and goals
- Gathering personal information, such as sleeping patterns and lifestyle information
- An explanation of how the hypnotherapy process will work
- Practical details, such as cost, cancellation policy, and how many sessions might be needed

Actual hypnosis generally starts in the next session. While the exact way in which this is done obviously varies from hypnotherapist to hypnotherapist, the structure below will give you an idea of what to expect.

- A welcome chat to encourage you to relax
- Induction – the hypnotherapist will lead you into a state of deep physical and mental relaxation
- Once deeply relaxed, the hypnotherapist can then begin to help you toward your goals, using the techniques and approaches he or she has discussed and agreed with you
- Once the above is completed, the hypnotherapist will begin the transition to wakefulness, in which you are gradually brought out of your trance
- Time for any questions you may have, a summary of the session and discussion of any progress made

How regularly you see your hypnotherapist will be something you will decide on together. Initially, you may decide you wish to meet on a weekly basis, but, depending on improvements and how you feel, you may choose to see him or her more or less frequently.

Is hypnosis all about belief?

Hypnosis enables you to move beyond any of your limited thinking and find within yourself everything you need to take your life to the next level of fulfilment. Put at its simplest, it is about helping people to believe different things about themselves very deeply. When a fully formed and powerfully positive image of oneself is absorbed deeply by the inner mind without any resistance, magical changes can happen very rapidly.

Belief is therefore everything. Even before hypnosis begins, a hypnotist will be working on your beliefs about him or her and about hypnosis in general. The effective hypnotist comes across as an expert who is confident, reassured and certain that what he or she does can have an impact on you. Above all, the hypnotist has to convince you that the hypnosis is going to work.

Can I be hypnotized against my will?

It is important to make clear at this juncture that if you don't want to be hypnotized you can easily resist it. And yet, even when a person wants to be hypnotized, it can still get complicated because the hypnotist has to stay in alignment with your beliefs, values and needs.

If a hypnotist tries to get someone to do something conflicting with their own values or goes against what is good for them, the rapport breaks down, the hypnosis dissolves and the ability to positively influence them disappears. That is one of the reasons there is a limit to what can be accomplished in a stage hypnosis show. The rapport and belief in an entertainment setting isn't usually deep enough to achieve truly transformational things. However, within a clinical context, once the subject and hypnotist have developed a good working relationship and the subject has already experienced significant positive changes in their lives due to the hypnosis, they then believe even more deeply. With that rapport and belief in place, the hypnosis can become all the more powerful.

While you can't be actively hypnotized against your will, and you certainly can't be made to do things that go against your ethics or values, it's important to recognize that you are being subjected to forces of persuasion every day which use very powerful psychological strategies to influence your choices. Learning more about how the mind can be affected by these techniques is a vital way of ensuring you are truly making your own decisions.

How can hypnotists put people into instant trances?

Picture the scene: a hypnotist stands on stage and invites someone from the audience to join him. Once he or she is up on stage, the hypnotist shakes the volunteer by the hand and then without any warning takes their hand and lifts it up to rest on their forehead. The hypnotist places his own hand on top and calmly orders his subject to 'sleep'. The volunteer goes weak at the knees and the hypnotist deftly lowers him or her down to lie on the stage floor to the amazement of the watching audience.

This appearance is deceptive. In fact, the subject remains fully conscious and is still completely in control. He or she is simply consenting to the experience. The hypnotist must have already created the necessary rapport during his initial presentation, and the subject is allowing the hypnotist to affect and lead him or her in this way. To get this far means the hypnotist has to operate with incredible skill. If a lay person were to try using the same methods and techniques, they simply wouldn't work.

Skilled hypnotists deliberately set out to build up an extraordinary amount of belief in their abilities. It is exactly this level of belief that is the key factor in making a hypnotist effective. Belief leads to the most powerful technique any hypnotist possesses: the power of what is termed congruence.

What do hypnotists mean by congruence?

When what we believe and what we say are totally aligned we are congruent, and when we speak from this place our words carry enormous power. In much the same way that people can tell when someone is lying, they also have a clear capacity to know when someone is telling the truth. However, there is a level beyond this.

When a person is absolutely convinced from the top of their head to the tips of their toes that truth is moving through them, when he or she is filled with certainty in every fragment of their being, congruence has been achieved. As far as the hypnotist is concerned, when he or she is certain that what you are doing is truly in your best interests, and when you are deeply in an authentic relationship with yourself, it is possible to communicate with a level of congruency that can be incredibly inspiring, uplifting and persuasive.

Congruent communication

This level of congruent communication is the magic ingredient in hypnosis, but it is also the magic ingredient of all communication. That is why I passionately believe everyone should make the effort to learn the main principles and practices of hypnosis because it furnishes you with such a deep understanding of truth, integrity and communication. It also gives you incredible leadership skills.

When you are totally clear about who you are, what you are doing, the approach you are taking, and it is absolutely crystal clear that you are operating with the best of desires to serve and lead others to the greater good, you will be amazed how people respond to you. They will naturally like and trust you and believe what you are saying more readily. You will automatically create a natural rapport with them before you have even said a word. When you speak, people will listen; when you ask them to take action they will stand up to be counted; they will believe they can make a difference, because your (congruent) belief in them will help them believe in themselves.

How do I find the right hypnotist?

Knowing what to do to truly help people when they are hypnotized takes a huge amount of training and skill. That is why it is very important to only work with a hypnotist that you know to be good.

The ideal is to work with a hypnotist who has been personally recommended to you by someone you know and trust. If this is impractical, using social media channels to find one is a good second best. In this case, the next thing to do is to have a conversation with your selection of possible therapists on the phone. If they are capable hypnotists, they should be excellent communicators. They should be able to put you at ease rapidly and sound very confident about their work. You should get satisfactory answers to all the following points:

- Are they a member of a recognized professional body?
- Are they subject to a formal complaints procedure?
- Can you call that body with a query or complaint?
- Where was their training and how long was it?
- Did they pass an independent examination?
- Are they committed to ongoing professional development?
- Is there a system of supervision?
- Do they have professional indemnity insurance?
- Do they abide by a written code of ethics?
- Is hypnosis their main job or is it a part-time hobby?
- How long have they been practising?
- How professional is their website?
- Do they have credible and reassuring testimonials?

It is also important to establish whether the possible hypnotists are happy, confident and successful. Are they healthy and in control of their lives? Are they an inspiration? Though this may be hard to ascertain over the phone, it is important to be very mindful about who you give permission to influence you.

This, however, is not about protecting you from actual danger. It is more about ensuring the success of the hypnosis, so that you have the best chance of getting the best result.

The greatest danger of working with a 'bad' hypnotist is that the hypnosis simply won't work and you will get no benefit from it. You may then walk away, dismissing hypnosis as ineffective without realizing you are turning your back on an incredibly useful tool. That is why it is important to work with

CASESTUDY THE HYPNOTIC POWER OF CONGRUENCE

A famous story about Gandhi highlights the power and importance of congruence. A woman approached him in the hope that he would speak to her son to get him to stop eating sugary cakes and sweets. She had walked for days to bring her son to meet with him and then waited patiently for hours and hours before finally gaining an audience with the great sage. Gandhi listened to her concerns and asked her to bring her son back again in a month's time.

Though pleased, the woman was a little frustrated. She had travelled a long distance and had to wait for a very long time before she could obtain an audience with the great sage. Sure enough though, a month later she and her son returned. Gandhi remembered her immediately and asked her to bring her son in. At that point he made himself as tall as he could and firmly placed both hands on the boy's someone who has been supporting himself or herself for many years as a full- time hypnotist. However, as this book demonstrates, the best hypnotist you will ever work with is yourself. You'll find out more about what makes it work in the next chapter.

shoulders. As he loomed over him, he ordered the boy with all the force he could muster to 'stop eating sugar'.

The boy was shaken to his core and pledged that he would do as he was told. He left the room, but his mother remained behind. She was pleased with the result but somewhat confused and more than a little annoyed. 'Why,' she enquired 'didn't you do that last time?' Gandhi smiled and replied 'A month ago, I was eating sugar'.

The moral is simple. When every part of us is aligned with truth, when we are certain of what we are saying, when we are absolutely convinced of the importance of what we are saying, and when that message is conveyed with love to someone in need of help, and they are receiving that message from someone they believe in, that message will go straight to their core and change them forever. That is hypnosis when it is at its most beautiful.

CHAPTER 2
How does hypnosis
really work?

In this chapter I want to share with you the fascinating, yet incredibly simple, truth about how hypnosis actually works. The first thing to note is that there are literally hundreds of different hypnosis techniques that a hypnotist may use depending on the effect he or she is hoping to create.

Before we start digging deeper into the world of hypnotic trance, I think it appropriate to begin by demonstrating how language and body language can influence us. Not only will this give you the tools to improve your own life, but it will also make it possible for you to better protect yourself from other people's influence and any possible attempts they may make to manipulate you.

How can people influence our behaviour?

There are three common ways in which it is possible to exert an influence on others, which we will explore one by one:

- Matching
- Pacing and leading
- Language patterns

Matching

When two people are getting along well together, a warm rapport develops between them. When this happens, it is common for them to unconsciously copy each other's body language. This is natural. When we unconsciously assess how other people are being, we unconsciously try to mirror them because we know that the more we are like them, the better chance we have of being liked and understood in return.

When ordering food in Indian restaurants, for example, I have to consciously stop myself from speaking with what could sound like a mocking Indian accent. I am not trying to cause offence. I am unconsciously trying to increase my chance of being liked and understood. Certain people, though, will deliberately use this technique to manufacture rapport. They will 'match' body position, tone of voice, speed of speech, vocabulary, class style, facial expressions and so forth to create a feeling of connection and closeness. With that 'rapport' it is easier to influence people.

Pacing and leading

Another way people can exert influence on others is by employing verbal statements that describe what another person is experiencing or believing. If you do this accurately, it, too, creates a feeling of rapport. It also sparks a conversational momentum that then enables you to steer people in certain ways. The technique is called pacing.

For example, you can ask someone three questions to which you know the answer is yes. With each yes answer you get, you build up some conversational momentum, which means it is much more likely that whatever you ask next will also be responded to with a yes. Technically, this is called a 'Yes set' and makes it far more likely that you will be able to get someone to agree to what you will be asking or suggesting next. That is called 'leading'. Together, both pacing and leading play a vital part in making hypnosis work.

A 'yes set' can also be created by simply making a series of statements that happen to be true. Let me try the following on you to demonstrate:

- So you are currently sitting or lying down reading these words (yes) (pacing)
- You can feel the book or electronic book reader in your hands (yes) (pacing)
- You are curious about hypnosis and how people can exert influence over others (yes) (pacing)
- While we discuss this, I invite you to please keep a really open mind (hopefully, yes) (leading)

You don't have to answer with an overt yes; the statements just need to resonate as true for you. The positive momentum this establishes is a powerful tool for influencing others and is utilized regularly in hypnosis. By building up a flow of 'yes' energy, you will be more open to where I am taking you.

Language patterns

Language patterns steer us every waking moment. When you become aware of how they work, it is amazing to discover how many people are trying to influence us. In hypnosis, they can help to take you into a trance and also help with the subsequent hypnotherapy, as you will discover if you are working with a therapist.

A good therapist will use language patterns to focus the attention and turn it inward to search for meaning. The language used is also permissive – that is to say, it gives you the maximum freedom to interpret what is being said to you in a way that makes the best personal sense.

If I was going to hypnotize you, I would start by explaining how hypnosis works. I would do my best to reassure you and do everything I could to get you to feel that I knew what I was doing, that I am a good person, and that I have your best interests at heart. Ideally, this creates *real* rapport, which is vital for the success of the process.

While there are covert language patterns and manipulative techniques that can exert an unconscious influence, hypnosis works best when you have obtained full permission from the person being hypnotized to influence him or her positively. With that level of agreement, it is much easier to create real, lasting changes to how a person thinks, feels, believes and behaves. With full rapport established, you are then able to use this way of leading people even more powerfully.

What are the main steps hypnotists take to put people into hypnosis?

Let me talk you through how influence and positive persuasion are used to take people into hypnosis so that they

---

FOCUSON FILTERING REALITY

The brain constantly filters reality, only letting us become consciously aware of things that fit our model of the world. For instance, you are not consciously aware of all the information that is entering your mind this very moment. While you have been reading, it hasn't been relevant, so your inner mind hasn't bothered to let you be conscious of it. It might be a car going by outside, the washing machine rumbling away in the background, or the feeling of your toes. Take a moment right now to focus on your toes and how they feel.

Such sensory feelings have been constantly reaching your brain but have been filtered out as described above.

---

can connect deeply with their own resolutions, their greatest potential and ultimately their own freedom. There are four main stages:

- Induction
- Deepener
- Resolution and post-hypnotic-suggestion
- Awakening

Hypnosis works in many ways by drawing your attention to what is already there. By bringing your attention to it, a hypnotist can invite you to bring relaxation there and to feel more positive feelings by becoming more aware of positive sensations. This not only induces relaxation but it also helps people become more aware of their previously unrecognized potential.

Where are your unexpressed gifts? What other aspects of your potential currently might not be a part of your conscious awareness? Maybe you have the capacity to be an amazing artist, an incredible snowboarder, a multi-linguist, a storyteller, an inspirational speaker, or even a gifted hypnotherapist? Hypnosis can lead you to discover innate capacity and capability that could astound you.

After outlining the purpose of each stage, I will give you scripts to enable you to practise these techniques on yourself and others. You can also go to www.freemindproject.org to watch videos of me putting people into hypnosis. There are recordings of the scripts there as well.

Preparation

Before beginning with the actual scripts, read the following to your subject:

'Just to be clear, this process is designed to help you feel very relaxed and positive. It is a gentle introduction to hypnosis that will involve four stages. Firstly, I will help you to enter into a simple hypnotic relaxation by inviting you to relax your body and deepen your breathing. The second stage will involve you going deeper into relaxation by increasing your awareness of your physical body sinking into a relaxed state. Then in the third stage I will give you suggestions for you to feel good about yourself so that you are in a good mood for the rest of the day. The final stage will then involve me gently bringing the whole experience to a gentle close.

'I will have no power over you. I cannot make you do anything against your will. While you are experiencing this you will remain fully conscious. This is not about going to some faraway place where you have no memory of what happens. This is about you becoming more aware and gaining more control of your life. I am simply here to help you connect with more of your potential. At anytime if you want to stop you can simply open your eyes. I recommend that you keep as still as possible, but if during the experience you need to rearrange your body or scratch an itch, that is fine. Do whatever you need to do to be comfortable. Please also be aware that it is normal to have a skeptical part of your mind questioning the process and analyzing your experience. Don't worry too much about that. Allow that part to continue and simply bring your attention back to what is being suggested to you.

'Most of all simply try to enjoy the process. If you can maintain a curious and open mind you may be amazed at the power you have to improve how you feel.'

The last thing you must do before you begin is to confirm permission to lead your subject in this process. Simply ask, 'Do I have your permission to lead you in this process?' Without such consent, the hypnosis will not work. Once this has been granted, understand sincerely that you are truly working for your subject. You are serving him or her, and every word you use in the script is being said for the subject's welfare. Bring as much care and attention to the process as you can as that will make the whole experience much more powerful.

Induction

If you came to see me for hypnosis, this is how I might induce you. I would start by asking if you would like to go into hypnosis sitting up or reclining on a couch, so embedding the idea that, either way, you are agreeable to going into a hypnotic trance. Next, I would invite you to stare at something in the room, really concentrating on it. Then I would ask you to think about your breathing patterns. I would get you to slow down your breathing, inviting you to breathe all the air out of your body, pause briefly, and then to breathe in fully, filling your tummy first, followed by your chest, and then pausing at the top of your breath before breathing out again.

With each out breath, I would then invite you to allow your eyes to feel more and more tired. I would tell you that, when you close your eyes, the feelings of relaxation would deepen immediately and that you would feel relaxation spreading beautifully down through your body. I would then watch to see your eyelids looking heavy and tired and I would simply say 'heavy and tired' in time with each of your out breaths. You would then usually allow your eyes to close after a few breaths. At that point I would say 'deeper and deeper, more and more relaxed as we continue.'

When our eyes shut, our conscious mind processing is reduced by about 30 per cent. This is a natural relaxant that is pretty much guaranteed. So now I can say, 'deeper and deeper as we continue' with complete conviction. Not only am I pacing your experience very accurately by saying this, but also by using the phrase 'as we continue' I am setting the expectation that the feelings will deepen further. Everything I will have said so far will have been true, so you will begin to believe what I am saying more and more.

Deepener

Once your eyes are closed and you are in a light hypnotic trance, I would start to describe the physical sensations associated with deeper states of relaxation. It is very common for people to think as though their body is heavy and tired, though some feel as if it is light and floating. It is also common for people's stomachs to gurgle as they relax. Drawing attention to these sensations increases the subject's awareness of the relaxation.

The skill of the hypnotist lies in the ability to describe what may be happening for you, taking care to include every possibility. So it is common for a hypnotist to say something like, 'You may notice that your arms and legs are beginning to feel very heavy and tired, you may also notice sensations of floating or lightness, or you might not yet notice the sensations of hypnosis moving through your body.' If you break this down, the hypnotist is taking care to cover *every* possible outcome.

The arms and legs may feel heavy, they may feel light, or, indeed, the subject may not have noticed any change at all.

Resolution and post-hypnotic suggestion

Once someone is deeply hypnotized, he or she is connecting to a very powerful part of the unconscious mind. Any positive and empowering suggestions offered at this time will be absorbed very deeply. It is also very common for a hypnotist to create suggestions that will be activated once the hypnosis is over and you emerge from your trance state.

It is worth bearing in mind, too, that when people are in this deep hypnotic state they will also naturally find answers to their own challenges, gaining great relief and insight about things that may previously have been troubling them for years. From a hypnotherapy point of view, once people are in this deep hypnotic state it is possible to employ a range of different techniques and practices to help them think, feel, believe and behave differently. There is more on this in subsequent chapters.

Awakening

Once a subject has been hypnotized and the purpose of the hypnosis session (relaxation, healing, insight, inspiration, improved performance and so on) has been accomplished, the hypnosis is brought to a close by bringing the subject back to full waking consciousness. This process usually involves bringing the subject's attention back to his or her body, getting them to maybe move their hands and toes gently while feeling they are integrating all the benefits from what they have undergone.

The awakening process usually involves adding in final suggestions for feeling good, setting up the subject to enjoy the rest of their day in a very relaxed mood. It is also a very useful way of helping people to get more familiar with the hypnosis state. Once the subject's eyes are open and they are sitting up, they often can recognize actually how deeply relaxed they were. It can be very convincing.

How can I hypnotize someone else?

Initially getting people into a hypnotic trance is relatively easy. Knowing what to do when they are hypnotized to create real and lasting change in their lives is much more complicated. Those powerful techniques are covered in the chapters that follow, but, to begin with, here are some instructions that you can safely use to put any willing friends and family into hypnosis by simply reading the instructions to them out loud, paying close attention to the additional guidance in brackets.

Hypnotists call these written instructions scripts. Starting on page 57 are scripts for:

- Inducing hypnosis
- Deepening hypnosis
- Giving someone positive suggestions to put them in a great mood
- Awakening them from hypnosis

Try these scripts on your friends and family and invite them to use them on you, too; the only prerequisite being the sincere desire to give your subjects a wonderfully relaxing and positive experience – as well as a desire on their part to be given such an experience, of course. This is the best way to start understanding the beauty of the unconscious mind and the simple, but profound, power of hypnosis.

Delivering the scripts

It is important to deliver the scripts very slowly and gently, speaking in a calm and soothing tone and really savouring the deeper meaning of each word. I also recommend that you allow yourself to drift into a very deeply relaxed state. The deeper you go, the deeper your subject will go.

As you read, pause whenever you see three dots. Really take your time over this. You need to give your subject time and space to notice and feel what you are directing them to be aware of. Place special significance on the **bold** and *italic* word as you utter it, invoking the essence of what the word means and suggests. There are also some extra instructions in brackets here and there to help with the delivery. I recommend that you read through the scripts and the additional instructions in advance so that you understand them fully before using them on someone else.

If you would like to experience this as a subject first, you can download a recording of the scripts being delivered by me from www.freemindproject.org.

Stage 1: A warm and gentle hypnotic relaxation (Induction)

'Make yourself **comfortable** and allow your eyes to stare at one point in front of you ... become totally **transfixed** on that point, just separate your hands and let them lie **loosely** in your lap ... or by your sides if that's more **comfortable** ... it's better if your legs are uncrossed ... but it doesn't matter ... if you feel you need to move just slightly, now and again **that is fine** ... you don't have to be **absolutely still** ... just be comfortable and relax your whole body as much as you can ...

' ... now bring your attention to your breathing and do what you can to **slow your breathing down** ... keep staring at that point even if your eyes **begin to tire** ... please keep your eyes open until I invite you to close them ... enjoy taking the time to breathe **all of the air out of your body**, breathing out for longer than you would usually ... pause before breathing in to notice **how relaxing it can be** to breathe that deeply ... when you breathe in, breathe in **slowly**, filling your lungs completely and **really enjoy the process** ... pause at the top of your breath ... before breathing out to really **enjoy slowing your breathing down** with each breath ...

'... notice how your eyes are probably getting a little heavy and tired ... wanting to close ... and when you want to **allow yourself** to enjoy **going even deeper** into this experience ... you will want to let your eyes finally close ... in the meantime just notice how with each out breath ... your eyes are getting more and more **heavy and tired** ... **wanting to close** ... **you may also begin to notice that your eyes are feeling blurry** ... like you are middle distancing and not really looking at anything in particular ... and so take a moment to feel the eyes getting droopy wanting to close ...

(Say the next suggestion as your subject breathes out) 'with every out breath **more and more** heavy and tired ...' (and again as they breathe out) '**more and more** heavy and tired ... and **NOW simply allow your eyes to close** ...

'... just allowing your whole body to relax as you do so ... **deeper and deeper**, more and more relaxed ... and just keep listening quietly to the **sound of my voice** ... as it helps you feel *more and more relaxed* ... you may well be aware of other sounds, too ... sounds inside the building, sounds from outside, maybe passing traffic ... but these won't disturb you ... in fact, they'll **help to relax you**, because just for now the world outside is absolutely unimportant to you ... the only sound you're interested in is the **sound of this voice** ... helping you to relax more and more with each and every breath ...

'... take a moment to notice how your body is beginning to feel very relaxed ... **you may notice** that your arms and legs are feeling very heavy and tired ... you **may begin to notice** that your body feels as though you are floating ... or you may have **not yet noticed** any of the feelings associated with **going deeply relaxed** moving through your body ... just notice what you notice now ... as we continue ... remembering to **pause before breathing in** ... and **pause before breathing out** ... and while you're listening to the sound of this voice ...

'... if your mind wanders at all don't worry, just bring your attention back to your breathing and concentrate on **slowing it down** even further, feeling more and more relaxed as the **feelings of relaxation** spread further and further down throughout your mind and body ...

'... breathing more and more slowly ... and as you breathe out each time, just allowing your whole body to **relax more** *and more* ... so that you gradually find yourself feeling more *centred, peaceful and focused* with each and every breath ... remember there is no right or wrong way to do this ... just notice what you notice and *allow this to be whatever it is* ... trusting that you will get from it what you need ...'

Stage 2: A wonderfully soothing deep hypnosis (Deepener)

'As you breathe I would like you to imagine that you have just stepped out in the morning and that it is a warm and *sunshiny summer day* ... take a moment to imagine that, as you breathe in, you are *breathing in warm sunshine-filled, blue-sky air* ... and, as you breathe out, imagine you are letting go of old and grey, tired clouds ... imagine your inner world becoming a bright blue sunshiny day and that with every out breath you are letting go of any stress, strain and tension from your mind and body ... feeling *more and more positive and relaxed as we continue* ...

'... in a few moments I am going to count down from ten to one ... *with each descending number between ten and one* allow yourself to notice deeper feelings of relaxation beginning to spread down through your mind and body ... maybe *imagine a sensation of peace spreading down throughout your whole body* with each descending number ... you may feel that as a *warmth starting* at the back of your neck ... or you may notice your hands and feet are *going to sleep* ... just notice what you notice as you allow yourself to enjoy this experience in whichever way *works best for you* ...

'... so with each descending number ... really allow yourself to deepen the experience ... take a moment now to *imagine* that *at the count of one* ... you will feel really *deeply relaxed* ... what would it be like to be that deeply relaxed? ... start to *feel the feelings* you would associate with that and allow them to be more noticeable as this experience continues ... *deeper and deeper* ... more and *more peaceful*, so ready ...

(In this next section say each number as your subject is breathing the last bit of air out at the end of each breath. Then wait two cycles of breath before you say the next number. So they breathe out, you say the number, then they breathe in, breathe out, breathe in and then right at the end of their second out breath, you say the next number in the sequence. Really take your time over this.)

'*10* ... (wait two breaths) *9 deeper and deeper* ... (wait two breaths) *8* ... (wait two breaths) *7* ... (wait two breaths) *6 more and more relaxed* ... take a moment to notice how *good it feels* to allow yourself to *enjoy* this experience *more and more* ... *and 5*, halfway down, deeper and deeper, the second half is much more noticeable, like a wise part of you is nodding its head in approval, *the deeper you go the better it gets* and the better it gets the *more you realize* that this is a place of *peace and power* ... *4 deeper and deeper* (wait two breaths) ... *3 more and more relaxed* ... (wait two breaths) *2* feeling more *peaceful and positive* (wait two breaths) ...

'... and *1 deep, deep down* ... *more and more relaxed* ... *deep, deep down* ... it doesn't matter where you go or where you drift, my voice will travel along with you, enabling you to enjoy deep levels of restorative relaxation ...'

Stage 3: Adding positive suggestions for a lovely day (Post-hypnotic suggestion)

'... take a moment to *allow your mind to wander* ... maybe drift off to a favourite *place of relaxation* ... or possibly a favourite holiday destination ... or *enjoy a positive memory* of a time when you felt *deeply relaxed and happy* ... make the imagery, sounds and feelings vivid in your imagination and be there now ... maybe thinking of a time when you had fun with friends ... or maybe a time when you *felt you had done something really well* ... it doesn't matter where you go or where you drift ... you might not think of anything specific at all ... simply allowing you to *enjoy positive feelings of relaxation in your body* instead ... your inner mind will choose the *perfect time and place* for you to connect to *positive feelings now* ...

'... *feeling peaceful and happy* ... really noticing the positive feelings in your mind and body increasing ... this will allow you to *feel more positive and relaxed over these next few days* ... take a moment to feel those *positive feelings in your body now* ... and now simply enjoy imagining yourself coming round from this experience *feeling really happy and positive* ... think about how that will benefit you and those that you care about ... as the days and the weeks go by you will *notice feeling more easily relaxed and happy* ... the more time you spend in connection with your inner mind ... *the easier everything gets* ...'

Stage 4: Regaining full awareness (Awakening)

'... in a few moments I am going to invite you to bring this to a close ... take a moment now to *let this experience be whatever it was* ... some of it may have been *easy and positive* ... other parts may have not worked for you at all ... *let it be as it was* ... trusting that with practice it can become more effective and enjoyable ...

'... in a moment *I am going to count up from one to ten* ... with each rising number you will feel *more peaceful and positive* ... you will feel more integrated and all normal sensations will be returned to your body ... every part of you will be back in the present ... and you will feel ... *good, relaxed and positive* ... ready to enjoy the rest of your day ...

'... take a moment to be grateful to your inner mind ... and if it feels appropriate promise to spend more time connecting with your inner mind in these next few months ... so ready, *feeling good and positive* ... slowly coming round but keeping your eyes closed until number 8 ... so beginning to count up ... *1* ... and *2* ... *coming round slowly*, feeling relaxed and positive ... being gentle with yourself ... 3 ... *feeling aware of your body ... slowly coming round* ... *4* ... nice *and relaxed*, feeling good ... *and 5* ... maybe gently moving your hands and toes but keeping your eyes closed ... *6 feeling good*, maybe beginning to stretch your arms and legs out ... 7 ... *feeling peaceful and positive* ... 8 ... *gently opening your eyes* ... 9 ... *all normal sensations returning to your body fully* ... *and 10* ... *fully back here in the present, every part of you back and feeling good.*'

How can I deepen my understanding of hypnosis?

The best way to advance your understanding of hypnosis is to experience it as much as you can and to practise hypnotizing others who are happy to explore the process with you. A vital part of this is to notice for yourself and to discuss with your subjects what worked and what didn't. Through those explorations and discussions you will learn about the power that language has to shape your experience. You will discover how effective even the simplest technique can be in helping yourself and others to feel very differently.

This, however, is just the beginning. There are lots of other incredibly powerful techniques that can be used when you are hypnotized that can make a huge difference to your life.

The processes that create change fall into three main categories: deprogramming, reprogramming and reconnection. Deprogramming is the process by which you systematically dissolve and let go of everything that is holding you back and skewing your perception; reprogramming is the term used to describe the embedding of new empowered and positive beliefs; while reconnection focuses on deepening your links to yourself and the world at large. The most popular and powerful tool within all of these ways of effecting change is visualization.

How does visualization work?

It is a fact that the body cannot tell the difference between imagined situations and real life. This is most noticeable in ourselves when we get nervous before an exam, job interview or first date.

When you start thinking about what lies ahead, your unconscious mind reacts as though you are already in that situation. It cannot tell the difference between reality or the thought of reality and therefore releases extra adrenalin in an attempt to prepare you for what it thinks is the immediate ordeal even though the actual one may be weeks away. When you use this kind of visualization technique during hypnosis the effect deepens profoundly.

Combining hypnosis and visualization also enables you to experience some of the benefits of the places that you love without even leaving home. Just by imagining yourself in

---

TRYIT VISUALIZATION IN ACTION

It will take you just a couple of minutes to test out how visualization works. Read through the instructions here and memorize them. Then put the book down and carry out the test from memory.

1 Close your eyes and take a moment to focus on your breathing, concentrating on slowing your out breath.

2 Now imagine yourself in your kitchen. Familiarize yourself with the feel of it, the look of it and even its smell. Take a minute or so over this.

3 Visualize yourself going to wherever you would keep a lemon in the kitchen, take a knife and cut the lemon in

---

such a place, your body releases the feel-good hormones serotonin and dopamine.

At the same time, the levels of adrenalin and cortisol in the body are reduced. This naturally reduces anxieties, increases feelings of rest and enables you to think peacefully about things that were previously stressful.

half. Once you have done this, vividly imagine raising the lemon to your face and smelling it. Then bite down on it and squeeze all its juice into your mouth.

4 Now open your eyes and continue to read ...

You probably noticed that, when you bit down on the lemon, you started to salivate; indeed, some people start salivating as soon as they even say the word lemon. What the exercise demonstrates is that the body will respond to what you visualize as though it were real.

Your body thought you were eating a lemon and it produced saliva to help you to digest it. If, however, I asked you to consciously salivate right now without imagining food, it is unlikely you could do it.

CHAPTER 3
What are the main
purposes of hypnosis?

Having explored in the previous chapter what hypnotists term the art of influence and how that is applied, I would now like to provide you with an overview of the following important applications of hypnosis. The examples below demonstrate just how broad these can be.

- Changing beliefs
- Altering perception and perspective
- Optimizing performance
- Enhancing rest and relaxation
- Managing fear
- Increasing motivation
- Boosting health and healing
- Enhancing other forms of therapy
- Deepening spiritual practices

I'll also address the following common question about hypnosis in order to debunk one of the more negative myths about the practice: can it be used to manipulate people?

How can hypnosis change beliefs?

Our beliefs totally determine our experience. What we believe about our abilities and about life has a huge impact on how we operate, what we expect and what we notice. In a way, our beliefs are filters through which we see the world. Like wearing sunglasses, our beliefs really affect what we see.

Hypnosis can help you to discover what your underlying beliefs really are. It can also help you look at the reasons you believe what you do and can work on changing these beliefs if they are limiting you. Most people never spend time exploring their beliefs to discover the possible limiting thinking that may be unnecessarily holding them back. Until Roger Bannister ran a mile in under four minutes, it was considered impossible. People had been trying to achieve this feat for decades without success. Yet, once he had done it, hundreds of people managed it over the following years.

Limiting beliefs prevent us from moving forward in our lives as well. What we believe is maintained in place by what we think about ourselves and what we tell other people about ourselves. These are called language patterns (see page 47). In some forms of hypnosis, it is common to get people deeply hypnotized and then repeat to them over and over again positive statements that will empower them to think more positively about themselves. This style of hypnosis is called direct suggestion (see page 26) and it can be very powerful. Most hypnotherapists use it during the final stage of a hypnosis session to help build the subject's confidence and general feelings of wellbeing and self-appreciation.

Frequently, hypnotherapists also suggest empowering sentences to their subjects for them to repeat throughout the day to help them work consciously on thinking, feeling, believing and behaving differently. These positive statements or sentences are often called affirmations, vision statements or mantras. It is easy to dismiss them as too simplistic, but don't make that mistake as using them to 'reprogram' yourself can have a huge impact on your life. Chapter 5 contains examples of vision statements you can start using to discover their power.

How can hypnosis change perception and perspective?

Obviously, how you think about things affects how you feel about them. However, as well as your opinions, beliefs and possible fears, there are other types of thinking processes that affect how you feel.

The way you make pictures in your mind as you think has a huge impact on how you feel. For example, if there is something you are afraid of, it often looms quite largely in your inner mind when you think about it. If you think about it with your eyes closed, the image that represents what you fear will most likely be big and sit in full colour in the centre and front of the mind. By using hypnosis techniques to shrink the image down and maybe shift it to one side, you will feel less anxious about it. You could then imagine draining the colour from the image or simply allowing the image to

FOCUSON KNOWING THAT OUR BELIEFS CREATE OUR REALITY

A wise old man is sitting on a bench outside his village when a traveller approaches him. The traveller tells the old man he is looking for a nice place to settle down. He asks the old man what the people are like in his village. The old man replies by asking the traveller what the people were like where he has come from. The traveller explains that they were mean and unpleasant. The old man sighs and says that the traveller would find the people in his village much the same. The traveller decides to continue his search elsewhere.

The next day, another traveller approaches and asks the same question. Once again, the old man asks him what the people were like where he has come from. The traveller replies that people there were kind and pleasant. The old man smiles widely and welcomes the traveller into the village, explaining that he would find most of the people there much the same.

The moral is simple. We find what we expect because what we see is a projection of who we are and what we believe.

disappear over the horizon, dissolving at the last moment into the sun. Or you could create a silly soundtrack and add a selection of odd noises to the image.

By altering seemingly small details like this, you are able to decrease any negative feelings and increase the positive ones. If you want to feel more confident, content and calm, changing the way you view yourself and the things challenging you inside your mind can be very effective in helping you to think, feel, believe and behave differently. When you do that, your perspective naturally widens and deepens, which generally puts you in touch with a much wiser way of seeing and doing things.

How can hypnosis enhance and optimize performance?

Many top performance coaches use hypnosis and visualization to help their clients perform at the very highest level. The potential applications are endless.

If, for instance, you panic at the thought of speaking in public, visualization can help to make you more comfortable with the process. Relax yourself first by going to see a hypnotherapist or by using self-hypnosis. Then simply visualize in your mind the speech going well. Just practising this over and over again can have an immensely powerful effect, as what you are doing is encouraging your body to feel more relaxed and content. The more you can get used to this, the easier it will be to draw on the power of the technique on the day.

You might also find that performing a symbolic physical ritual – something as simple as punching the air, say – will help to put you into the perfect frame of mind. It is commonplace, for instance, to see sportspeople performing such a ritual before they make a putt at golf or take a penalty at football.

Another example of performance enhancement dates from the 1980s, when the US Army became disappointed by the average standard of its soldiers' ability to shoot after their initial training. The celebrated performance coach Anthony Robbins used visualization and empowered language patterns to get the soldiers to think, feel, believe and behave as though they were effective marksmen and their performance greatly improved as a result.

Most of us, however, remain unaware of how our daily thoughts and associated actions are programming us and therefore our performance in everything we do. Hypnosis enables us to become more conscious of these thoughts and so purposefully direct our psychology to support us positively in all our endeavours.

How can hypnosis be used to enhance rest and relaxation?

Using hypnosis to aid rest and relaxation has all sorts of positive benefits. What you will be doing is utilizing what experts call the relaxation response. Though there are various ways of achieving this, visualization is undoubtedly one of the best. All you need to do is to create mental pictures that are so captivating, rich in detail, powerful and all-consuming for

3 Untwist your body and come back to the centre with your hands down by your sides. Now look over your left shoulder at the position you just pointed toward.

4 While still looking over your left shoulder, imagine doing the exercise again. Believe for a moment that, because you are engaging the power of your mind, this next time you will go further round. Pick a new target accordingly and take a moment to see and feel yourself pointing at it. The more you believe it, you will find the more it will come true. You might want to close your eyes to help you to imagine the scenario more vividly.

5 Come back to the centre, twist your right arm around to the right and see how far you get. Repeat steps 3 and 4. Then try again and see if you can go even further.

your mind that you end up getting lost in the imagery your mind is creating. This enables you to think more peacefully about things that previously were making you feel tense and stressed. If you are suffering from emotional distress, for instance, relieving it like this will encourage you to become more empowered. Achieving this empowerment wll help you to permanently resolve the issue, release tension and achieve a state of calm contentment.

Physically, relaxing like this has many benefits. Slowing the heart rate, for example, gives the heart a rest. Your blood pressure will go down as you slow the rate of breathing. Mentally, getting the emotional centres of the brain to rest gives the thinking part of the mind the chance to work as it should. Your ability to concentrate and solve problems will be boosted as a result.

How can hypnosis be used to manage fear?

It is common practice to expose people suffering from a phobia of something bit by bit to the thing that scares them. Take someone with arachnophobia (an irrational fear of spiders) as an example. The standard treatment starts with the therapist showing the sufferer a small black-and-white photograph of a spider, followed by larger, more colourful photographs and then a small plastic model spider. Finally, the sufferer is shown a real spider that is small and dead, and then a live spider. This process, called desensitization, can take a long time to accomplish. However, using visualization during hypnosis can often speed things up considerably, with the process of imagining the spider substituting for the photographs or fake spiders.

In much the same way, visualization during hypnosis can help people cope with more abstract fears about everything from exams and driving tests to first dates. The possible applications are endless. Imagine, for instance, that you are afraid of flying. To help you to overcome this, a hypnotherapist might start off by encouraging you to visualize travelling on a plane and then discussing how you felt while doing this. He or she would then investigate further to get to the root cause of the fear. This might involve asking where and when the fear first developed, whether you were alone or if someone else was with you and so on. The hypnotist would then steer you toward adopting new patterns of behaviour and teach you relaxation skills to help you to avoid becoming tense and stressed in the future. The aim is to create a positive energy within you that is stronger than the negative energy of your fear.

How can hypnosis be used to increase motivation?

Hypnosis can help you rediscover joy and inspiration in life, put an end to procrastination, turn mountains into molehills and reprogram yourself with the inner drive you need to progress towards the things you want to achieve. Once again, visualization plays a key part in this process.

Many hypnosis sessions will end with a hypnotist asking you to conjure up a compelling vision of your future. He or she will invite you to spend time in it and encourage you verbally to think about the beautiful place where you will be living, taste the glorious food you will be enjoying, marvel in the gorgeous views, feel in your body how happy and content you are, hear the kind of positive things people will be saying about you and, most importantly, embrace all of the positive things you will be feeling and thinking about yourself. It makes this kind of life seem more normal, thereby giving people hope, courage and the determination to continue pursuing their goals, whatever they may be, without feeling bogged down or frustrated.

How can hypnosis be used for health and healing?

A combination of hypnosis and visualization can provide extremely powerful support for the body's healing processes. Various scientific studies support the notion that, through the use of visualization, we can stimulate the body's natural defences against disease.

In 1985, Professor G Richard Smith, a psychiatrist at the University of Arkansas, published the results of experiments involving people using visualization to imagine their bodies attacking the chicken pox virus. The results showed that visualization accelerated the body's healing response, clearing the chicken pox more rapidly. In addition, using a combination of deep relaxation and positive suggestion to counter excessive stress and stimulate relaxation has been shown to lower bodily levels of adrenalin and cortisol, which, if present in excess, can adversely affect the immune system.

Stress also reduces the body's production of interleukin-2, a natural cancer-fighting protein that supports the activities of white blood cells in their response to cancer cells.

Hypnosis is also extremely effective when it is employed to relieve pain. In 2003, for instance, *Gut*, an important British medical journal, published the results of a study involving 204 people suffering from irritable bowel syndrome. The treatment consisted of 12 weekly hypnosis sessions, each lasting for an hour. Some 58 per cent of the male participants and 75 per cent of the female ones reported significant symptom relief immediately after finishing treatment. More than 80 per cent of those who reported initial symptom relief were still benefiting up to six years later.

Both hypnosis and visualization have also been used successfully by sportspeople to reduce recovery time after injury and to keep fit while they have to rest their bodies. The British athlete Steve Backley, the one-time world record holder for javelin throwing (he won the title twice), used visualization while his throwing arm was in plaster. He practised throwing his javelin in his mind three times a day. When the plaster was removed, his doctors were amazed at how little his muscle mass had reduced. It looked to them as if it had been well exercised. His recovery time was also much shorter than had been expected.

These are just examples of the ways in which the use of hypnosis can promote good health. As well as generally helping you to lead a more relaxed and therefore healthier life, an experienced hypnotherapist will be able to help you explore ways of coping with more specific health and wellbeing issues.

How can hypnosis be used to enhance other therapies?

Therapy in this context is defined as the understanding, treatment and relief of psychological and emotional distress or disease. Most people go to see a therapist – of whatever kind they choose – because they simply don't feel good, don't like the way they are thinking or because they find their behaviour is getting in the way of them enjoying their lives.

In simple terms, therapy is all about helping people to think, feel and behave differently. Most commonly, what makes the process work involves helping a person come to understand why they are thinking, feeling and behaving in the way they do. Once our conscious and, more importantly, our unconscious motivations are understood, it is much easier to make changes and enjoy life more.

Traditional (non-hypnotic) talking therapy is in many ways a very thorough process of systematically analyzing and improving how you operate in the world by gradually making you more and more aware of what you are doing and why. However, what is sometimes easier and quicker than talking, thinking and analyzing your challenges at the conscious level, is working directly with the unconscious. This is where hypnosis comes into its own. It can:

- Enhance communication between the conscious and unconscious mind
- Rapidly locate and uncover old thoughts and feelings that are causing difficulty
- Increase emotional objectivity and improve resilience
- Make people much more open and willing to revisit and heal past pain and trauma
- Bypass the limiting beliefs of the conscious mind
- Enable new and empowering beliefs to be accepted by the unconscious mind more rapidly

This makes hypnosis not only a wonderful form of therapy in its own right but also a potentially invaluable complement to – and accelerator of – other forms of therapy. Anyone who practises clinical hypnosis does so in the belief that people possess many more internal resources than they consciously realize. The role of the hypnotherapist, therefore, is to help them to discover and explore the resources within themselves and so enhance their innate abilities.

CASESTUDY REACHING A DEEPER LEVEL OF UNDERSTANDING

Lots of people focus on what they think is a problem without realizing that this 'problem' might be a symptom of a deeper fear. For example, I once worked with a woman who, on the face of it, seemed to be suffering from agoraphobia (the fear of leaving home). She was understandably deeply upset and saw the condition as being responsible for everything that was holding her back. It was only through deeper investigation that we were able to discover what was really going on beneath the surface.

While in her conscious mind my client longed to be in a relationship, her unconscious mind was scared of intimacy, rejection and being hurt. Her agoraphobia was simply a tool her unconscious was employing to keep her single. Our work together focused on resolving her fears about being in a relationship. Once those fears had been worked through and she felt willing to be open to a relationship, the agoraphobia disappeared. It is clear from this just how incredibly effective hypnosis can be at discovering what is really happening beneath the surface.

Can hypnosis be used for deepening spiritual practices?

There are many different belief systems and cultures in the world with widely varying notions of how best to live and how to be happy. Many of those belief systems have different ideas about life, religion, spirituality and the purpose of life.

Some people believe very strongly in the idea of a God, or gods, while others do not think of themselves as being religious but still consider themselves to be 'spiritual'. For example, some people may be passionately atheistic yet still employ traditionally spiritual practices, such as meditation or mindfulness, to help them feel more relaxed and confident. Such rituals are simply techniques that any person may use to help them enjoy their life more. For some people this might mean connecting more with God, while for others it could be about connecting more with nature or their own heart.

When you understand the principles and techniques of hypnosis it is possible to deepen these practices so that you can get more out of them. For instance, hypnosis can be used to:

• Relax your body so that you can meditate more deeply
• Centre your awareness so that you can be more mindful
• Increase your awareness so that you can be more present during the day

- Think more objectively about your identity and conditioning so you feel more free
- Increase your ability to be resilient in the face of difficulty
- Connect you more to your sense of understanding, sympathy and compassion
- See other people's perspective and be more forgiving
- Help you feel more accepting and loving of yourself

TRYIT **ACCESSING THE UNCONSCIOUS MIND**

The unconscious mind is full of great potential and capacity, but we don't always know how to listen to it. This exercise is intended to show you how it is possible to communicate directly with your unconscious to unlock your inner wisdom and potential so that you can enjoy your life more. It works best if you are deeply hypnotized, but, even if you are not, it is well worthwhile experimenting with it.

1 Allow your eyes to close and gently let your breathing slow down. Do your best to relax your mind and body deeply.

2 Imagine entering a sun-filled clearing in a beautiful forest. Take a moment to notice all the colours, sounds and smells and for a while enjoy the warm sunshine playing on

- Connect you more to nature and a sense of harmony
- Make your prayer time feel more profound
- Help you feel more grateful for the life that you have
- Overcome fear and resistance so you can have more faith in yourself and life
- Change how you think, feel, believe and behave so that you can love life more

your face and the warmth of the sun on your body. There are no distractions. There is not a cloud in the sky.

3 The clearing is where you are going to meet up with your 'wise council', a group of three or four people you respect and admire. They could be actual people you know and love, or they could be historical figures like Einstein, Gandhi and Mother Theresa. You can ask them for advice. You might have a specific question you want help with, or maybe you are simply looking for some general guidance.

4 This should be allowed to happen as naturally as possible. You should not worry if you don't see everything in full detail all at once. Ask your question or state your challenge and let the different characters speak to you one by one, each delivering their own pearls of wisdom.

Though some people may receive direct guidance from their 'wise council' (see box on page 87), you may not. Instead, you may find yourself simply thinking or daydreaming about your situation. Either will help you to understand why you are doing what you are doing, or help you to strategize how to do things differently. Hypnosis can deepen your experience of life in so many ways that whether you think of it as spiritual or not isn't especially relevant. What is relevant is how happy you are.

Can hypnosis ever be used to manipulate people?

Thankfully, there are limits to what hypnosis can be used to achieve. During the Second World War, for instance, there was a concern that hypnosis could be used to turn people into unwitting spies or assassins. It was thought possible that a secretary, say, could be hypnotized to respond to a code word so that just before delivering a cup of tea (or more likely a large brandy) to Winston Churchill, someone could telephone the secretary, say the word and turn an otherwise loyal employee into a mindless killing machine.

Military intelligence agencies actually experimented to find out if hypnosis could be used like this. It was discovered that people cannot be hypnotized to do things against their own will. If something clashes with a person's value system, the suggestions will not work. Anyway, if you have followed the guidelines on page 38 on how to find a qualified, experienced, well-respected, authentic professional hypnotist whom you trust and feel aligned with, this is something you need not worry about during your sessions.

Sadly, some of the underlying principles of hypnosis can be used in everyday life by some people to manipulate others to a certain extent. Examples include unscrupulous salespeople, seduction experts more generally known as 'pick-up artists' and con artists. Whether such techniques are used to sell ideas, politics, products or services it is important to be aware of how people are trying to get us to do what they want. We may feel at the time that our needs are being met, or our dreams are being given a chance, but it pays to be very mindful of the techniques people are employing to hijack your choices.

In general, though, the positive benefits of hypnosis far outweigh the negatives. It can help you unlock your inborn creativity and curiosity and can help you come to terms with your underlying worries and fears. Used properly, it can help you to programme the unconscious mind to develop empowering beliefs, so ensuring that you are the architect of your own destiny and the master of your fate. As you will discover in the next chapter, it can be the key to bringing about a host of changes for the better in your life.

CHAPTER 4
Can hypnosis change your life?

As we have already discussed, hypnosis is a tool that can enable you to be better at understanding yourself so that you are able to overcome your challenges more rapidly, achieve your goals more easily and enjoy greater levels of health, happiness and harmony. That can have a hugely positive impact on your life. In this chapter, we will look at what this means in practical terms regarding the actual difference you could be experiencing on a daily basis. Here, below, we will discuss how hypnosis can give you more of the traits and why that can be wholly beneficial.

- Becoming more resilient
- Bringing greater clarity to life
- Becoming a more compassionate person
- Gaining more integrity
- Becoming more courageous
- Increasing creativity
- Feeling more 'present' in each moment

You may well have other things you want to explore. For this reason, it is best to come prepared with a list of the questions and concerns you want to raise when you first consult a hypnotherapist. It is helpful to try to rank them in their order of importance for you. You should look on a hypnotherapist as a coach and guide who is there to help you through a combination of instruction and suggestion. Each hypnosis session is a partnership. The hypnotherapist contributes his or her skill and experience; you bring knowledge of yourself and the things you want to change and alter.

Do not be surprised, by the way, if the hypnotherapist asks you to do some homework between sessions. The exercises that follow in this chapter are all things you can do on your own to help increase your feeling of empowerment. It is also a good idea to keep a journal so that you can record changes as they occur.

Can hypnosis make you more resilient?

Hypnosis is a wonderful tool for deepening your ability to be more resilient in the face of difficulty. Because of the associated relaxation and the increased objectivity about what you are feeling and why you are feeling it, hypnosis enables you to work through the layers of your emotions quickly. This helps you to understand yourself and others more deeply, as well as helping you to let go of any hurt and deal with the defensive responses and negative reactions that usually make difficulties more pronounced and prolonged.

Hypnosis enables you to be more centred and calm when other people may get very distressed, scared and angry. This resilience, for example, will enable you to be more loving with your partner when he or she is having a bad day, calmer and settled when threatened or challenged, more able to present and perform under pressure and generally feeling more at peace with yourself and life as a whole. It is something that will come more and more easily to you as you practise and hone your hypnosis skills.

TRY IT LOVING WHAT IS

This exercise is designed to achieve and support a way of being that will give you greater resilience and enable you to enjoy everyday life, and all the positive things it has to offer, to the full.

1 Start by taking a moment to get relaxed and comfortable. Then stare at something. Do your best to become transfixed by really concentrating on it as hard as you can.

2 Gently slow your breathing down, making each breath last for as long as possible. Let your eyes feel heavy and tired and, when you are ready to relax, let them gently close.

3 Concentrate on your breathing even more, focusing on breathing all the air out on the out breath and breathing in fully on the in breath. You might also consider pausing

You can take as long as you like over this. Don't worry if your mind races off, disagrees or is judgemental about you and your experience. Simply focus yourself by bringing your attention back to your breathing and give all your experience (including anything negative or difficult) your full permission

gently before you breathe in and again before you exhale. This will help you to relax and enjoy the exercise even more.

4 Carry on doing this for a minute or so, ensuring that you remain completely comfortable. Then simply repeat to yourself in your mind the affirmation 'I completely accept this moment as it is.'

5 Do this slowly and gently for a minute or so. Then change the affirmation to 'I totally love this moment as it is.' Repeat this slowly and gently, again for a minute or so. Then change the affirmation once more to 'In this moment I totally love myself and the whole of life.'

6 Then simply allow everything to be as it is for a minute or so. Enjoy dropping all your ideas about the way a part of you thinks a thing 'should' be. Do your best to experience loving everything as it is.

or blessing. Allow yourself to be more curious, relaxed and welcoming to the whole of life and you will feel more at peace with yourself.

Can hypnosis bring greater clarity to life?

One of the biggest challenges that people face in life is not being clear about who they are, what they want and what they are doing. The more you can use self-hypnosis or work with a hypnotherapist to understand yourself more deeply, the better able you are to truly know yourself, your motivations and your real needs.

Without this awareness, it is possible for you to be following a career path that doesn't satisfy you. You could be overly materialistic, even though you know 'things' don't make you happy; or you could be confused about why, when everything is going so well, you don't feel so happy on the inside. Hypnosis is a tool that can help you establish real clarity about what you are feeling and why you are feeling the way you do. With that awareness it is easier to make sure your life is a true reflection of who you are and what you really want.

Can hypnosis make people more compassionate?

When you use hypnosis to work through the different layers of what you are feeling, it is not long before you realize that, underneath all of your challenges, dysfunctions and difficulties, it is always some kind of fear that is the actual, underlying problem.

Fear drives all disruptive and negative thoughts, feelings and behaviours. While this does not excuse bad behaviour, it certainly explains it. Realizing this can have a profound effect on the level of understanding and compassion you feel for others as well as yourself. Through this deeper understanding, you are able to be much more generous and kind to other people who are suffering and also to have more understanding for people in such situations. Treating people with compassion is the quickest way to get to resolution. Once you have seen this work a few times, it will deepen your belief in the transformative power of compassion.

Can hypnosis give people more integrity?

As you become more self-aware through using hypnosis, you become much more conscious of what feels good in your life and what doesn't. Pretty soon you realize that being true to yourself through being open, authentic and honest is the best way to build a life worth living. When we operate with this kind of integrity everything gets better. Hypnosis is a powerful tool in helping you to discover this. Every time you work on an emotional difficulty, sadness, a disappointment or a frustration with a hypnotherapist during a session, you will see that any

TRY IT **REBALANCING BELIEFS**

It is possible to speak to different aspects of yourself to bring balance to your beliefs and your choices. This exercise involves you working on the part of you that tells you that you need material things to be happy. If you would prefer to talk to another part of yourself that you feel could be more in balance – your appetite, for example – that is also fine.

1 Take a moment to get relaxed. Then find something to stare at and do your best to become transfixed.

2 Gently slow down your breathing, making each breath last for as long as possible. Let your eyes feel heavy and tired and, when you are ready to relax, let them gently close.

3 Then concentrate on your breathing even more. Notice the air coming in and out of your body and concentrate on breathing all of the air out on the out breath and breathe in fully on the in breath. You might also want to pause gently before you breathe in and then again before you breathe out. Do this for a minute or so.

4 Now imagine yourself to be in a beautiful clearing in a forest. Take some time to build up your sense of it by

focusing on the associated colours, sounds, sights and smells. I recommend filling the clearing with warm golden sunshine. You can hear the sound of running water nearby, the gentle call of birds and the rustling of leaves. You can even feel a gentle breeze on your skin.

5 Invite the part of you that you have singled out to come and sit with you. This part may look like you, or it might look like someone completely different. It could also appear as an object or a symbol.

6 Don't worry if you can't visualize this vividly. Without any mental imagery at all, you can still imagine having a deep conversation with this part of yourself. Then simply let that part feel appreciated. Thank it for its desire to help and nurture you, and then simply ask if it would be willing to bring itself into more balance.

7 You might ask this part what it needs from you for it to feel comfortable changing its ways. You can talk to yourself and negotiate with it, or you can simply rest in appreciative peace with it, trusting that the balancing is happening naturally just by going through the process. During this exercise, don't be surprised if you start thinking and planning new ways of being.

lack of integrity in your own actions or in the actions of others is harmful in some way or other.

As well as making this much more obvious to you, hypnosis also gives you the tools to dissolve the negative thoughts and feelings that make it more likely you will behave outside your integrity zone. Happiness comes from being able to put your head on the pillow at night feeling proud of who you are and how you are. The more integrity you live with, the better your life will become. People will trust you, while you will be more reliable because you will be much more likely to do what you say you are going to do. People will know where they are with you and you will be much clearer about where you are with you. This makes life infinitely easier.

Can hypnosis make people more courageous?

As you get more in touch with the innate wisdom of your unconscious mind, clearer about who you are and what you want, and really see the value in being true to yourself, it is most likely that you will begin to feel more courageous and confident in being yourself to the full. It can take real courage to do what is right, to stand up for what you believe in, or simply to be appreciated for what you are. The more you can do this, the more you will find people responding positively to you. This will inspire you to be even more self-expressed. In turn, this makes it much more likely that your life will soon become a positive and more rewarding reflection of who you truly are.

Hypnosis can deepen the permission you give yourself to truly live the life that you really want, to approach the people you want to befriend and to ask for your needs to be met. It does this by dissolving the thoughts, feelings, beliefs and behaviours that are holding you back and also by deepening your ability to see the benefits of living your life to the full. It is possible for a hypnotherapist to give you a vibrant and exciting glimpse into the beautiful future built on values, integrity, accountability and excellence you could create for yourself. It can also help you boost your performance and your abilities so that you can begin to believe more strongly that you can turn your dreams into reality.

Can hypnosis help people to be more creative?

As explained on page 25, the deepest level of hypnosis is called the Theta state. When you reach this level of relaxation, it is like inducing a waking dream. In this, you may experience wild and wonderful adventures that can be huge in scale and strangeness. It is a demonstration of the inventiveness of the subconscious mind.

The subconscious is an incredible tool that can be harnessed to help you respond more creatively to life. As already discussed, it is possible for you to become locked into certain ways of thinking, being and doing. Hypnosis can help you to counter this. The more you use it, the more flexible you can become in your approach to life. It can help you connect to different aspects of yourself that previously may have gone unrecognized, and it helps you bring more of the genius of the unconscious mind into your life in all kinds of creative ways, whether it is writing more effectively or creating a striking painting. You will become less rigid in the way you think and react to events as well.

Can hypnosis help people feel more 'present' in each moment?

As we have already established, hypnosis deepens our sense of self-awareness, but it can also be about deepening awareness of – and therefore acceptance, appreciation and enjoyment of – what is happening in the immediate moment, whether that is playing with your children, talking with your partner or even just doing the weekly grocery shop.

Many people spend their time busily rushing around, constantly thinking about what is next, overly dwelling on the past and then planning, strategizing or, worse, worrying about the future. When you can put a stop to this and instead become more aware of the present moment, you will find yourself connecting to a source of much greater happiness

TRYIT **GETTING OUT OF YOUR COMFORT ZONE**

Making a habit of pushing yourself to confront your fears and developing your courage is the best way to bring more happiness into your life. The human desire to be safe and comfortable is understandable, but unfortunately those conservative energies can hold in place all sorts of limiting ideas and beliefs we have about ourselves.

By choosing to do things that you wouldn't usually do, such as public speaking, mountain climbing, trying a new food or making small talk with a stranger, you automatically change your mindset. Being bold and trying new things naturally evolves your identity because it widens your idea of yourself, deepens your love for yourself, and connects you with a life force that can light up the world.

Your comfort zone holds in place everything that is holding you back. Getting out of this is therefore probably one of the most powerful life-changing practises there is. You are more capable than you can possibly imagine. If your ultimate potential could speak to you, who would it ask you to enjoy being today?

and effectiveness. This 'being present', or 'presence' as some people call it, is also referred to as 'being in flow' or being in 'flow states'.

The celebrated US psychologist Dr Martin E P Seligman, the founding father of the Positive Psychology movement, has

TRY IT MODELLING BEHAVIOUR

If there is someone you admire who is particularly good at something you would like to be better at, this exercise will help you to bring out the latent potential inside you.

1 Close your eyes and relax your body by deepening your breathing. Slow everything down and focus your mind. Do this for a minute or so to get deeply relaxed.

2 Then take a moment to imagine a situation where you would like to have more of a particular skill, ability or characteristic. You could call to mind a real situation from your past, or you could imagine a hypothetical scenario.

3 Invite the person you admire or respect to join you and visualize them managing the situation or demonstrating

carried out extensive research on the 'flow state'. His findings demonstrate that this is an extremely powerful tool that can help us enjoy life to the full while performing at our best. When you are 'in flow,' or achieving 'presence', everything takes on a richness and fullness that can make even the most seemingly tawdry moment exhilarating.

their ability. Take a moment to really enjoy watching them buckling down successfully to the task.

4 Rewind the scene to the beginning and float into this other person's body. Imagine being them and being aware of everything they think and feel. Take a moment to re-experience the situation as them, with all of their grace, ease and skill. Just simply enjoy experiencing that emotionally without knowing how.

5 Repeat the experience a few times and then ask that person to give you some advice about the things you could change in your life, or how you could approach this kind of situation differently. You might imagine them vividly talking to you or you could find yourself daydreaming all sorts of new ways to think and feel about this situation or this new skill set. Take some time to simply enjoy feeling more capable in this area.

'Presence' betters your ability to do everything. It is a state of deep, effortless involvement – the key to becoming more fulfilled and achieving your true potential. As you focus on a particular activity, your sense of self vanishes and time seems to stop. Athletes refer to this as being 'in the zone,' while others term it meditation or mindfulness. You are almost on automatic pilot as the power of your mind flows freely through you and all your feelings, thoughts and actions.

Over recent years, the number of people practising mindfulness on a daily basis has become extraordinary. Its popularity stems from the fact that it is so easy to do while its benefits are immediately tangible. After practising it, you are likely to feel more contented within yourself and able to concentrate more easily on the things that are really important to you.

Put at its simplest, the practice of being mindful is all about becoming more conscious and aware. A hypnotherapist will help you to focus concentration on the present moment, and regular hypnosis can help you to enjoy being much more present throughout the day. This will help you to identify the opportunities that surround you as you start programming yourself for success. As you will discover in the next chapter, self-hypnosis can also play an important part in enabling you to achieve this.

TRY IT A MOMENT OF MINDFULNESS

In recent years the number of people practising mindfulness on a daily basis has increased enormously because it is both so simple to do and delivers immediate benefits. Here's how:

1 Sitting upright in a straightback chair, close your eyes, stay very still and deepen your breathing.

2 Let your hands rest comfortably in your lap. Take a moment to settle, then gently open your eyes and soften your gaze.

3 Notice one thing about the room you are in – the colour of the walls, say, or the texture of the flooring. Close your eyes and then notice one thing about your physical sensations – the feeling of your spine or the soles of your feet.

4 Open your eyes again and repeat as many times as you want. Afterward notice the difference you feel. You are likely to feel more contented, concentrating more easily on the things that are really important to you and ready to seize the day.

CHAPTER 5

How can you make self-hypnosis part of your daily life?

Self-hypnosis is an extraordinary tool you can use to help enjoy much more happiness and success in your life. It is frequently employed to modify behaviour, emotions and attitudes. It can be a real help in dealing with the problems of everyday living. It can boost self-confidence and help you to develop valuable new skills. A great stress and anxiety remover, it can be used to overcome bad habits, such as smoking and overeating, as well. Always remember there are many ways in which you can help yourself through self-hypnosis. After all, you know yourself far better than any hypnotist could ever know you.

What are the benefits of self-hypnosis?

You can use self-hypnosis simply as an enjoyable way of accessing a peaceful, relaxing place, to calm yourself down if you are feeling particularly stressed or upset, or to access other positive emotions to help you to modify behaviour. Access different memories to help you feel more calm, secure and at ease in different situations. Before making a presentation, for instance, you might want to spend time enjoying a memory of a time when you presented something really well or were very funny and entertaining. You can also use self-hypnosis to reconnect with the early days of a relationship to reinvigorate the love you feel for your partner. Or you could improve your relationship by simply connecting to a time when you felt especially happy and attractive.

How do people hypnotize themselves?

What follows is a simple three-stage self-hypnosis technique that you can practise regularly on yourself. It can take a bit of practice and feel quite odd when you first get started, but you will quickly improve. Do your best to be patient, open-minded and creative. The fourth stage is optional. It will help you to improve your performance in any area of your life, but you should try it only once you feel confident with the first three stages.

When you are starting out, it can be useful to enlist someone you trust to read you the instructions the first few times, so that you can keep your eyes closed. Alternatively, you can download a recording from the FreeMind website that will talk you through each of the stages and then teach you how to use the techniques for yourself, just click on www.freemindproject.org. This way, you still benefit from the power of practising hypnosis at home but without the pressure being on you to be both therapist and subject.

Preparing for a session

It is important to make yourself comfortable before you start a hypnosis session at home. As well as this, you should ensure that you won't be interrupted by anyone for the duration of the session. For this reason, it may be better to do the exercises either first thing in the morning or last thing at night.

The three stages here plus the optional one can all be completed within 20 minutes. The first three stages take around 15 minutes, while, if you simply want to try out stages 1 and 2, it will take only ten minutes. Ideally, you should also leave an extra five to ten minutes free afterward for further relaxation and/or contemplation.

During the exercises, it is normal for your mind to wander so do not worry if this happens. Other than that, adhere to the following guidelines and you will most likely not only manage to hypnotize yourself easily but also discover how enjoyable the process can be:

- Do the exercises with your eyes comfortably shut
- Keep yourself as still as you can – you can move if needs be, but after readjusting yourself get back into stillness
- You may find some parts of the exercises easier than others, but don't worry as there is nothing you can get wrong
- Don't get frustrated with yourself or think that these experiences have to be anything in particular
- Keep an open mind as it is normal to have doubts – simply be curious about what is happening
- Try each exercise at least twice

You may notice that, at times, certain exercises won't work at all for you. In this case, repeat it later or try a different exercise, and you may respond differently. As you get further into the session, you may notice strange sensations, such as heaviness or lightness, starting in your body. You may even feel as if your whole body is going numb. These are all perfectly normal reactions. You can stop whenever you want and your body will rapidly begin to feel 'normal' again.

Stage 1: Relaxing into a hypnotic state

Self-hypnosis works best when your mind and body are completely free of tension, so follow the steps below to achieve this.

1 Take up a comfortable position, either sitting up or lying down. Gently close your eyes. Then focus on slowing your breathing down. Exhale all the air out of your body, gently pausing at the end of each breath before inhaling the next. If, like most people, you find it difficult to let go of all of the air, you need to concentrate on letting it out gently, flattening your belly toward your spine.

2 When you breathe in, do so slowly and fully. When your lungs are full, gently pause before breathing out again. Make each breath last as long as possible. This will slow your whole system down. If your mind wanders, bring it back to notice the feeling of your breathing slowing and deepening further.

3 Consciously try to relax every part of your body. You may want to start at your feet or head, and then simply breathe out. Allow each part in turn to feel valued and thank them for all that they do for you. Concentrate on holding positive feelings for each part of your body, making sure you include your head.

4 Once you are physically relaxed, picture yourself in a place of great natural beauty. It could be somewhere you know well, such as a vacation destination, maybe a fantasy island, or an imaginary woodland paradise. It should be a place that feels good and happy. Think of the colours, the sounds, the tastes, the smells, and the textures that you would experience there. Change your clothes in your mind to suit the place you are imagining and imagine yourself being there as vividly as you can. At the same time, allow a feeling of relaxation and gratitude to move gently through you with your ever-deepening breath. Centre yourself in the experience and enjoy it as much as possible.

If you decide to end the session now, simply bring things to a close by letting your attention return to your body. Wiggle your fingers and toes and let your eyes open again. If not, continue with the next stage.

Stage 2: Deepening your experience of self-hypnosis

The more deeply hypnotized you are, the more your connection to your unconscious mind will open and the more possibilities there will be for positive transformation in your life.

What follows here is one of the most popular techniques for inducing deeper levels of relaxation. It is the same method as described in Chapter 2 (see page 60), the difference being that now you are not being talked through the process by a hypnotherapist. Read through the instructions carefully and remember what you need to do. Otherwise, ask a friend to read the instructions to you, or download the recording from the website: www.freemindproject.org/what-is-hypnosis.

1 If you are starting from scratch, induce a simple hypnotic relaxation using the breathing technique described in stage 1.
2 Tell yourself that you are about to count from ten to one and that with each descending number you will go one-tenth deeper into relaxation. Tell yourself that by number five you will be halfway down and really enjoying it and that, once you get to number one, you will be really deeply relaxed.
3 Take a moment to imagine being deeply relaxed with each number. Then, take another moment to imagine being completely relaxed by the time you have counted down to the number one. Look forward to that feeling and expect each number to relax you more and more.
4 Soften all of your muscles and let all the tension out of your mind and body with each breath you take.
5 When you are ready to begin the countdown, simply count the numbers down in your head very slowly. The best time to say each number to yourself is at the bottom of the out

breath when you are letting go of all the air out of your body. This is naturally relaxing.

6 Begin with the number ten and count down to one, but, before counting down to each successive number, take two more long, slow breaths. At the end of the second out breath, resume the countdown. Really take your time over this.

7 Take two more long, slow breaths and at the end of the second one, count down to the next number.

8 Continue counting down at the end of each second out breath with the last bit of air. Each time you say a number, pause to feel its effects. You should sense everything slowing down and becoming more peaceful.

9 With each descending number, tell yourself that you are going even deeper into relaxation.

10 During the second half of the countdown, after the number five, your body will feel much more relaxed. At the count of number one, notice the very deep level of relaxation flowing through your mind and body.

11 Now, just enjoy the intense feelings of relaxation as they continue to deepen.

To bring this stage to a close, count up from one to ten. Tell yourself that with each rising number you will feel more aware. Then slowly begin counting, focusing your attention on your body. Wiggle your fingers and toes at number six and gently open your eyes when you reach number eight. As you say the numbers nine and ten familiarise yourself with the room you are in. You will be back to normal waking consciousness, feeling fully present and positive. Otherwise, ignore this instruction and proceed to stage 3.

Stage 3: Empowering yourself to change your life

As discussed in Chapter 3 (see page 75), the use of positive language patterns to focus on parts of your character or capability that you want to improve is the key to making changes in your life. Repeating the following statements to yourself – either out loud or silently – while you are hypnotized (and therefore highly suggestible) is a very simple and yet powerful way of freeing up more of your potential.

You can either keep your eyes open to read the whole list or simply memorize two or three of the statements that you feel would be particularly useful. These statements are also included on the recording on the webpage www. freemindproject.org if you would rather listen to them until you feel comfortable saying them yourself.

Though, on the face of it, this process may appear to be too simple to have much of an impact, do not underestimate its power. Simply reading the whole list last thing at night and first thing in the morning (whether hypnotized or not) is a wonderful way of setting yourself up for a beautiful day. If you feel that any of the statements are not relevant to you, simply skip them. Similarly, if you feel you would like to add more of your own, feel free to do so.

Whichever route you take, the statements need to be honest, positive and simple. Being honest is extremely important. If you try to plant things you really do not want to do or achieve into your subconscious, you will not be successful. The statements should be straightforward – not more than a few words. Just say them to yourself quietly several times over.

1 Each and every day, I am feeling more and more confident

2 Each and every day, I believe in myself more and more

3 Each and every day, I accept myself more and more

4 Each and every day, I am enjoying feeling more and more fun and playful

5 With each day that passes, I am more and more capable of seeing the positive in all things

6 With each day that passes, my listening skills are improving

7 The more I like myself the more I like my life; the more I like my life, the more I like myself

8 I am feeling more and more relaxed, each and every day

9 Each and every day, I am finding myself to be more and more motivated

10 Now I see all responses to me as opportunities for growth and learning

11 The more open I am, the more open I am to positive empowering change

12 Each and every day, I am becoming more and more aware of the benefits I offer to others

13 With every moment that passes, I am finding more and more ways to earn money

14 By day and by night, all my affairs are prospering

15 I am pleased with my natural ability and I trust myself more and more

16 Each and every day, my ability to enjoy every area of my life is improving

17 I am rich in spirit; I am rich in ability; I am wealthy

18 By day and by night, I am discovering new levels of happiness and contentment

19 Each and every day, I am improving myself in each and every way

20 Each and every day, I am being more and more compassionate/supportive/engaging/inspiring (use any word you want)

21 Each and every conversation, I am speaking more and more effectively/dynamically/assertively (use any word)

22 With every moment that passes, I am more and more compassionate and open with myself and others

23 Each and every week, I am running my business/department/work (use any word you want) more and more effectively and smoothly

24 Each and every night, I am sleeping more and more deeply and getting more rest, leaving me more and more energized every day

25 Each and every day, I am treating my body with more and more respect

26 By day and by night, I love my body more and more

To bring this part of the session to a close, simply count up from the number one to the number ten as before. Or, if you decide to continue, you can use what follows to bring out your best from yourself

Stage 4 (optional): Using self-hypnosis to enhance performance

There will always be times when you are put on the spot – in exams and interviews, or during dates and meetings, for example. The visualization exercise that follows (which refers to whatever situation you are preparing for as the 'challenge') is designed to help you ensure that you have the best chance possible of being at your best.

1 Follow the guidance in stages 1 and 2 to achieve a deep state of hypnosis

2 Follow the guidance in stage 3 to put yourself in a positive frame of mind, using as many or as few of the vision statements as you want

3 See yourself just before the challenge looking confident and happy

4 Visualize yourself taking three magically relaxing deep breaths in and out

5 Try not to worry too much about the result. Relax and suppress any 'neediness' as best you can

6 Take three deep breaths, relaxing more and more with each one

7 Envisage entering or beginning the challenge looking calm and collected, breathing slowly and deeply

8 See yourself at the end of the challenge with it having gone well (don't define that too much)

9 Enjoy the imaginary experience, feeling proud and positive about how well you did

10 Repeat the following vision statements, feeling positive emotions as you repeat them:

- Each and every moment, I am more relaxed about everything that happens.
- Each and every day, I am enjoying being myself more and more.
- Each and every day, I am feeling more and more confident and capable.

11 Bring yourself out of hypnosis, using the method described at the end of stage 2.

Do this as often as you like. Then, when it comes to the time of the actual challenge, take three deep breaths, feeling each breath have a magical relaxing and positive effect on you, before beginning it. You might also want to repeat the three statements I have provided above at this point. All of this will put you in the best possible frame of mind to ensure that you perform at your best.

Accepting and being yourself is the secret to success, but it can take practice to build up the courage to do this. This exercise is full of techniques to help you achieve this more and more. After a while, you'll find that it becomes second nature to expect things to go well. This type of self-hypnosis can really help you to stay calm and be at your best when it really counts.

Deeper and better

Remember that the more you can deepen hypnotic relaxation, the more you open up the connection to your subconscious mind. The more deeply hypnotized you are, the more effective all of the other hypnotic techniques you may employ become. Therefore, spend some time practising, taking yourself into hypnosis as deeply as possible. All you then need do to ensure progress is to relax and concentrate on a specific area, and you should obtain immediate and noticeable results.

TRYIT DEALING WITH INSOMNIA

If you are prone to sleeplessness, you are not alone. Self-hypnosis can help you to overcome the problem and fall into a deep sleep that should last through the night. Try this simple four-step sequence:

1 Progressively relax your muscles while also focusing on breathing slowly, deeply and naturally.

2 Visualize yourself in a tranquil place, such as a mountain meadow filled with wildflowers or a quiet tropical beach.

3 Continue breathing deeply and slowly, keeping your thoughts focused on the image in your mind.

4 Tell yourself that, as you relax, you will drift comfortably into a satisfying slumber from which you will wake up refreshed the following morning.

Alternatively, counting sheep makes use of two powerful aspects of hypnosis – visualization and the mantra-like repetition of numbers. For it to be really effective, count backward rather than forward.

CHAPTER 6

Can hypnosis help make
the world a better place?

People in the developed world are richer than they have ever been and yet studies show that they are less happy than ever before. The UK and the USA score terribly on national levels of happiness, with both countries breaking records for the prescription of anti-depressants. It is not uncommon in the USA, for instance, for three-year-olds to be prescribed anti-depressants.

One of the main problems, as I see it, is that many people are looking for happiness and success in all the wrong places and ways, by which I mean outside of themselves – by 'buying' things, 'achieving' things and so forth. Whereas, in reality, happiness and success begin and end within our own minds – they are internal constructs no amount of external 'stuff' can build.

We each have the capacity to create the perfect life for ourselves that could fulfil us beyond our wildest dreams. Firstly, though, we need to connect with our hearts and innately wise unconscious minds in order to define what this is. What would make you truly happy? Why are you doing what you are doing with your life? Is it about immense wealth, fancy clothes, luxurious holidays, enduring fame and fantastic adventures? Or, underneath all that, is it more about the quality of your own thoughts and acting in alignment with your own morals and values?

How can hypnosis help us remove 'shoulds'?

Hypnosis is an incredible tool that can be used to help you move beyond your conditioned idea of what you 'should' do or what your life 'should' look like. Through it, you can dissolve the social conditioning that may have you convinced that you are not satisfied unless you own the latest phone, the fastest car or a pair of shoes for every occasion.

You can use hypnosis to give you the courage to venture into your past and release old and limiting thoughts, feelings, beliefs and behaviour. You can bring yourself naturally into harmony and you can develop the skills to start living life in ways that will make you much happier and more successful.

If more of us regularly engaged in positive self-development techniques such as hypnosis, not only would our levels of self-awareness be enhanced but so, too, would our awareness and understanding of others, whether people, animals or nations. This would lead to increased compassion in all our actions, both micro and macro.

Our greatness exists inside us. All the difficulties that come our way are actually opportunities for us to discover greater and more beautiful ways of being. I believe that it is likely that if more people learnt the simple principles and practices of hypnosis, many of the world's troubles would greatly diminish.

Not only would the internal struggle with depression and anxiety subside, but so, too, would the external battles for territory, resources and control. Happiness and harmony could be reclaimed as our natural state, because what is true for the individual is also true for society as a whole: our happiness is the world's happiness. Our world would then be an infinitely more beautiful place to live.

How can hypnosis be used to make people happier?

Every day we find ourselves at a crossroads. We have the choice to move toward truth, freedom, love and happiness, or we can move toward pretense, restriction, fear and unhappiness. Sometimes the crossroads appears as a massive life decision and yet in other moments it appears in minor decisions that we have to make or difficulties that we have to face.

The two paths

Whether the situation is big or small, we always have the choice to move toward truth, love and freedom. When we do that, things generally get easier. There is a flow to life and things tend to work. People want to be around you, they warm to you rapidly and they believe in you more readily. I call this the 'efficient' path. However, if when faced with a difficulty or a disappointment we contract, hide from the truth, opting instead for pretense, false politeness, or, worse still, deceit, we move away from who we really are. Fear takes more of a hold and we increase the need for control. Logic takes over and our heart closes bit by bit.

I call this the 'educational' path because, if we continue moving in that direction, things stop working. Life gets difficult. People don't like us or trust us. Everything has to be planned. There is no space for true creativity or fluidity. Life becomes rigid and joyless. The loss of happiness is an important message worth listening to, but many people are not paying attention to this warning sign. If we are lucky, it will help us see that something is off key and out of alignment.

Ideally we then reconsider and bring ourselves back into balance, but, if we do not, the 'education' gets more pronounced. What began as an absence of joy and happiness can then deteriorate into more prolonged feelings of anxiety and depression. If that doesn't wake us up to the importance of changing, then the lessons (messengers sent to remind you to live with more truth and joy) get more noticeable. Then it is common for people to experience all kinds of other difficulties.

If someone hasn't been listening to the messages and hasn't been taking appropriate action, he or she usually starts making bad choices. Over time, that can lead to unhealthy lifestyles, reckless risk-taking and sometimes even criminal activity or directly anti-social behaviour. If you allow yourself to reach rock bottom, everything falls apart.

Of course, such situations are exceptionally distressing, but what if such experiences are simply a type of message to let you know that the way in which you have been living is out of alignment. What if all of those disasters were simply an attempt to encourage you to re-establish harmony?

In so many ways, the modern world is out of alignment with natural wisdom. There are lots of 'messages' asking us as a society to consider doing things in different ways to prevent things from further 'falling apart' – protests (political corruption), floods (environmental negligence), disease epidemics (overuse of antibiotics), riots (social inequality), schoolchildren shooting at their fellow students (wholesale disenfranchisement of the young), huge increases in mental health medication prescriptions (low national happiness), insane levels of busy-ness and other addictive behaviour (disconnection, dissatisfaction and denial). All of these point to problems in how we are living as a society.

How can hypnosis help us re-establish alignment?

The story of the phoenix rising from the ashes is a well-known concept in Chinese mythology. It is a metaphor for the process of healing that takes place after things have fallen apart. What is less well known, however, is that the phoenix that rises from the ashes is only one part of the metaphor. The phoenix has a brother who also has a highly important role to play.

According to the original Chinese tale, when something or someone was out of balance, there were two firebirds that could restore the status quo. It was thought that a person or society would be sent messages warning them to change their ways. If, however, those messages were ignored and balance was irrevocably lost, then the first of the firebird brothers – the dragon – would descend from the heavens, burn everything to the ground and so destroy all the structures that were out of balance. Then, out of the destruction, the phoenix of harmony rose from the ashes, its tears having the capacity to heal any and all wounds. It is interesting that although most people in the developed world are familiar with the phoenix, the dragon brother has been lost somewhere along the way.

Hypnosis helps you get to the phoenix phase much more quickly because it is the tool that enables you to hear the message long before anything needs to be destroyed. When things go to the bad, or if you really hit rock bottom, if you have the courage to truly feel despair, that pain is full of guidance and growth. It is a whispered memory of who you really are. It is your potential waking you up to yourself. It may well be outwardly awful but these disasters are often blessings in disguise.

When people ask me to make their lives better, they often present me with a 'problem' or 'disaster'. I know that the dragon has burned through these areas of their lives with the best of intentions and that with a bit of courage, plus a willingness to shed some healing tears, they, just like the phoenix, will rise, reborn from the ashes, fully alive and living in ways that are much more in alignment with who they naturally are. From there natural happiness arises – no chasing or creating required.

The more people there are in the world living and loving their lives to the full in this way, the much happier the whole world can become.

Is there a link between hypnosis and enlightenment?

How you feel about life is your choice. Right here and now, you could define love, happiness, gratitude and peace in such a way that would enable you to experience everything and anything you want to feel. You could define success as having more money than you could ever spend, being super fit and having great relationships with everyone in your life.

You could also define success as being lucky enough to take your next breath. Your definition is your choice, but what you decide and what you believe changes everything.

Across the ages, all the world's cultures and wisdom traditions speak about an extraordinary way of being that is filled with peace and power. It has gone by various names and is described in many different ways, but essentially I am talking about enlightenment. The principles, practices and benefits of hypnosis are mirrored in its principles, practices and benefits. Understanding this is the key to understanding how we can change the world for the better by using hypnosis to raise our emotional and psychological awareness.

The world without enlightenment

Unfortunately, the developed world's model of civilization further compounds our territorial, competitive and possessive animal instincts, so we are tuned to interpret reality from a fear-based survival perspective. When fear and resentment are running the show, we are much more likely to harbour grudges, make snap judgements about other people and fall out with friends and family members.

Work is more likely to be a struggle, and we may be more likely to stress out about money when we don't have it – as well as more prone to stress about it when we have plenty of it. Going out may feel like a threat or a chore because it is easier to avoid interaction. People may feel like nuisances to be avoided and, very often, we see others as simply a means to an end. The world becomes more cold and aggressive, and we become more and more closed and hardened. Inevitably, this means avoiding real intimacy, and thereby living half-filled lives with half-told truths and half-lived dreams.

The foundation of happiness

You will enjoy life more after freeing your mind of all doubts, imagined inadequacies, grudges, and grumbles; letting go of a painful story if you feel you have one; dropping any feelings of having been a victim; relaxing your need for control; and stopping trying to manipulate yourself and others. When we drop our resistance to life, even in the most difficult of times, we discover a huge capacity to be at peace. Developing that capacity to relax into the flow of life and to bring a deep and strongly held sense of yes to everything is essentially what enlightenment is all about.

This is the foundation of all happiness. When we are free from over-identification with our personal story, we can begin to relate more freely to every moment. Our potential is given the chance to truly shine through, and thus many of our limitations, which previously restricted us, dissolve. We become free in the moment with the result that we become playful, positive, passionate, and alive. When we experience ourselves as whole and complete, and love ourselves unconditionally, we can finally let other people be who they truly are as well. When we can love everyone else unconditionally, we become someone that brings out the very best in others. We become a blessing in our own lives and most certainly a blessing in the lives of others.

Absolute or unconditional happiness is the capacity to be at peace no matter what is going on around you. You feel good because of who you are, not because of what you do or what you have. When you can free yourself, even just for a moment, from the idea that something external is the key to your happiness you begin to access a peace and contentment that dwarfs all your other experiences.

Is there a link between hypnosis and spirituality?

Spirituality is about finding what lights you up, moving beyond your negativity and fear and letting yourself and your brilliance shine brightly. In order to express your greatest gifts and create a life that truly reflects who you are, however, you need to be able to know how to create real and lasting change in yourself and the way you do things.

This is what hypnosis can help you achieve. It gives you the deeper psychological understanding you need to actually change behaviour. Otherwise you might have the deepest spiritual intentions to live life in accordance with your integrity – you may be committed to being a loyal and faithful partner, for example – but when it comes down to it, you fail to live up to the standards you set yourself.

Bringing hypnosis and spirituality together

Spirituality without the effective psychological tools to dissolve negative thoughts, feelings, beliefs and behaviour can be awful, with people witnessing themselves repeating the same destructive and limiting life patterns time and again. However, psychological awareness also needs to be grounded in a deep spiritual understanding, or people use the powerful tools of change to create lives they think they want without that vital understanding of real happiness and success. Such people can make amazing things happen, but very rapidly their life comes to feel pointless. In brief, spirituality without psychology is a blunt tool that won't create change, and psychology without spirituality never leads to real happiness.

Hypnosis brings psychology and spirituality together. With its help, you can access the most powerful part of your mind while also grounding it in a heart-centred awareness that means you have the ability to change combined with an insight into what is truly good for you and those around you.

FOCUS ON ACHIEVING 'COSMIC CONSCIOUSNESS'

Hypnosis is the quickest and most effective way of imprinting changes in behaviour, attitudes, beliefs and feelings on the subconscious mind and so helps to open the gateway to spiritual enlightenment. It can be used to achieve what Dr Ronald A Havens, a Professor of Psychology at the University of Illinois, defines as 'a state of cosmic consciousness'. According to Havens, 'experiencing just one of its aspects can trigger all the other aspects of that state of mind, culminating in a cascade of events that eventually lead to the full experience.' In the trance state, hypnotic suggestions are employed to create the kinds of thoughts and sensations that typically occur during what Havens terms 'a mystical state of enlightenment'.

It is therefore the ultimate tool for helping individuals enjoy more happiness and success in their lives, while also making it much more likely our world is becoming a more kind and considerate place. Imagine a world filled with empowered and joyful people, all lovingly engaging in life in meaningful, productive and positive ways – what a wonderful world that would be! Hypnosis could be the key to achieving it.

What next?

To conclude, I would like to suggest some of the things that you can do next to enjoy discovering more about hypnosis. Start by continuing to experiment with all the 'Try it' boxes in this book and also the scripts and step-by-step guidance in Chapters 2 and 5. For the sake of ease, all of the exercises, hypnosis scripts and step-by-step guidance are also available in one place on www.freemindproject.org, along with tutorial videos to help you get the most out of the experiences. While many of the exercises are simply an introduction to hypnosis, you are likely to be amazed at the degree to which even such simple techniques can enhance the way you are feeling and the way you therefore experience life.

As well as experimenting with the relaxation and positive suggestion techniques on your own at home, do look into reputable hypnotherapists in your area and decide who might be best to work with you on whichever areas of your personal and professional development you most feel you need help with. All of the top performers in the world of business and sports work on developing their inner mind to help them bring out their very best, so why not afford yourself the same luxury by investing in making the most of your potential? You will get a huge return on your investment by seeing – and feeling – improvements in every area of your working and emotional life.

If, after all of the above, you feel by any chance that hypnosis is something that you may like to pursue as a career – to help others with personal transformation as well as yourself – I cannot recommend it highly enough. It is so rewarding to help people overcome their difficulties, achieve their goals and help them enjoy greater health, happiness and harmony. After just one week of professional training you could have developed the basic skills to stop people smoking and help them overcome phobias and fears. To do more advanced work you would, of course, need much more training, but within just a year you could have an established practice working on the full range of challenges your subjects may present. If you are already a counsellor, a therapist or a coach of some kind, adding hypnosis to your armoury of tools can be a hugely rewarding way to broaden what you have to offer.

Above all, remember that hypnosis is the one way of getting the unconscious and conscious minds working in harmony. In fact, it is the most useful tool we possess for bringing about lasting change at the subconscious level. Through it, you can really empower yourself to change every aspect of your life for the better. I hope this book has inspired you to begin exploring the power of your subconscious because I know that, when you do, you will be amazed at the extraordinary potential in you that is just waiting to be released.

Further Reading

Allen, Roger P. (2004). *Scripts and Strategies in Hypnotherapy.* Crown House Publishing.

Bandler R. Roberti A, Fitzpatrick O (2013). *The Ultimate Introduction to Nlp.* HarperCollins.

Battino R, South MS & Thomas L (2005). *Ericksonian Approaches: A Comprehensive Manual.* Crown House Publishing.

Chopra, D. (2008). *Ageless Body, Timeless Mind: A Practical Alternative to Growing Old.* Rider.

Fortes Mayer, T (2014). *The FreeMind Experience: The Three Pillars of Absolute Happiness.* Watkins Publishing.

Gawain, S (2002). *Creative Visualisation.* New World Library.

Grinder J, Bandler R, Satir V and Bateson G (1989). *The Structure of Magic 1.* Science and Behavior Books.

Hamilton D (2008). *It's The Thought That Counts: Why Mind and Matter Really Works.* Hay House.

Havens Ronald A and Walters C (2002). *Hypnotherapy Scripts: A Neo-Ericksonian Approach to Persuasive Healing.* Routledge.

Heap M and Aravind K (2001). *Hartland's Medical and Dental Hypnosis.* Churchill Livingstone.

Murphy, J (2007). *The Power of Your Unconscious.* Wilder Publications.

Robbins A (2001). *Awake the Giant Within.* Simon & Schuster.

Robbins A (2001). *Unlimited Power.* Simon & Schuster.

Wolinsky S (2007). *Trances People Live.* Bramble Books.

Acknowledgements

I would like to take this opportunity to thank the hypnotists who have inspired me the most. Milton Erickson, Ormond McGill and Stephen Wolinsky have taught me in very different ways the power of language, belief and the possibility of rapid change. I would also like to thank my colleague Zoe Clews and her wonderful associates who I practise with in Harley Street. The dedication and care that is brought to every client continues to inspire me every day.

Thanks must also go to my publishers for asking me to write this book, my second for them. That thanks includes everyone who has been involved in the process of bringing the book to life, but special thanks must go to Kelly Thompson for her dedication to getting things right and the care with which she managed the process. Much gratitude must also go to Jeremy Harwood and his wife Sarah Bloxham, who were responsible for the Herculean task of helping me wrestle a vast subject into this short volume.

Thanks must go as well to the people to whom I have taught hypnosis. Working with individuals who have a passion for learning this beautiful art form so they can help others transform their lives brings me extraordinary pleasure. Much love and thanks must also go to Rhia Pratsis and Virginia Thorn for their endless encouragement, support and love. Finally, I want to thank my wife Anna, my daughter Portia and my son Theo for inspiring me and loving me as I am. You make it all worthwhile.

ABOUT THE AUTHOR

TOM FORTES MAYER

A Harley Street hypnotist and happiness author, Tom Fortes
Mayer has built up a worldwide reputation for his powerful
work. He believes passionately that hypnosis is the key to
rapidly achieving real and lasting change. In addition to his
private practice, he is also the founder of the FreeMind Project
charity, which aims to bring more happiness to the world.
He also runs a Hypnosis Training Academy, where his
greatest passion lies in teaching other people to
become ethical, highly-effective hypnotherapists.
To find out more about the Academy, go to
www.freemindproject.org/hypnotherapy-training.

ABOUT THE SERIES

We hope you've enjoyed reading this book.

If you'd like to find out more about other therapies, practices and phenomena that you've heard of and been curious about, then do take a look at the other titles in our thought-provoking **#WHATIS** series by visiting www.whatisseries.com

#WHATIS

The growing list of dynamic books in this series will allow you to explore a wide range of life-enhancing topics – sharing the history, wisdom and science of each subject, as well as its far-reaching practical applications and benefits.

With each guide written by a practising expert in the field, this new series challenges preconceptions, demystifies the subjects in hand and encourages you to find new ways to lead a more fulfilled, meaningful and contented life.

OTHER TITLES IN THE **#WHATIS** SERIES:

What is a Near-Death Experience? by Dr Penny Sartori
What is Sound Healing? by Lyz Cooper
What is Numerology? by Sonia Ducie
What is Post-Traumatic Growth? by Miriam Akhtar
What is Mindfulness? by Dr Tamara Russell

WATKINS

Sharing Wisdom Since
1893

The story of Watkins dates back to 1893, when the scholar of esotericism John Watkins founded a bookshop, inspired by the lament of his friend and teacher Madame Blavatsky that there was nowhere in London to buy books on mysticism, occultism or metaphysics. That moment marked the birth of Watkins, soon to become the home of many of the leading lights of spiritual literature, including Carl Jung, Rudolf Steiner, Alice Bailey and Chögyam Trungpa.

Today our passion for vigorous questioning is still resolute. With over 350 titles on our list, Watkins Publishing reflects the development of spiritual thinking and new science over the past 120 years. We remain at the cutting edge, committed to publishing books that change lives.

DISCOVER MORE...

Read our blog

Watch and listen to
our authors in action

Sign up to
our mailing list

JOIN IN THE CONVERSATION

 WatkinsPublishing    @watkinswisdom

 watkinsbooks   watkinswisdom   watkins-media

Our books celebrate conscious, passionate, wise and happy living.
Be part of the community by visiting

www.watkinspublishing.com